H. A Rudall

Beethoven

H. A Rudall

Beethoven

ISBN/EAN: 9783742881670

Manufactured in Europe, USA, Canada, Australia, Japa

Cover: Foto ©Thomas Meinert / pixelio.de

Manufactured and distributed by brebook publishing software
(www.brebook.com)

H. A Rudall

Beethoven

The Great Musicians

BEETHOVEN

By H. A. RUDALL

LONDON
SAMPSON LOW, MARSTON, SEARLE, & RIVINGTON, Ld.,
St. Dunstan's House
Fetter Lane, Fleet Street, E.C.
1890

RICHARD CLAY & SONS, LIMITED,
LONDON & BUNGAY.

CONTENTS.

NOTE.

It would have been impossible to enumerate systematically year by year the works of so prolific a composer as Beethoven without turning this little biography into something like an extended catalogue. Instead, therefore, of crowding the pages with titles, dedications, and opus numbers, it has been thought well in most cases to mention such compositions only as were connected with external events of more or less importance in the composer's career, and to refer the reader to the end of the book for a complete list of Beethoven's printed works. The ample materials for such a compilation, which exist in Nottebohm's catalogue and elsewhere, have been already turned to the best possible account in the Appendix to the *Dictionary of Music and Musicians;* and the writer offers his cordial thanks to Sir George Grove for kindly permitting this to be used as a basis for the Catalogue here given.

London, February 1890.

BEETHOVEN.

CHAPTER I.

ATTEMPTS to trace the ancestry of LUDVIG VAN BEETHOVEN have been successful so far back as the middle of the seventeenth century, when a family bearing that name, and related to the composer, lived in a small village near Louvain, in Belgium; and it was at about that time that one of the members quitted his village home and settled in Antwerp. Documentary evidence no less authoritative than the parish register shows that in 1685 the Beethovens were residing in the ancient city; the migration having, as a matter of fact, taken place some thirty-five years before that date. There the composer's grandfather—also named Ludvig Beethoven—was born. In the qualities of energy, independence, and musical ability early manifested by this progenitor, persons fond of tracing the influence of heredity in the lives of the world's greatest men—a subject very frequently illustrated in the pages of musical biography—will find material ready to hand. Whether or not Ludvig quarrelled with his family, as has been supposed, it is known that he quitted Antwerp at an early age, that when about eighteen he was among his Louvain connections, and that for about three months he occupied a post as singer in one of the churches there. On the expiration of this temporary engagement he sallied forth once more to fight his battle with the world. Whither to turn his footsteps was a question there can have been but little difficulty in deciding. Naturally and irresistibly he was drawn to Bonn—at that time the centre of attraction for all young and ambitious musicians, and the seat of the great art-patron Clement Augustus, Elector Archbishop of Cologne.

The position filled by these ecclesiastical princes was in some respects a peculiar one, involving important privileges, but not the title of majesty. Their principal function is explained by the word "Elector." With them rested the right of electing the emperor or king during the period when Germany was an elective monarchy. They were nearly always connected with the reigning family, and the splendour of their courts, the munificence of their patronage, which on the whole was intelligently directed, drew within their circle most of the leading spirits in art, science, and letters. Their priestly vows seem to have sat rather lightly upon them; and some notion of the relative importance attached by them to ecclesiastical and social duties may be derived from certain items in the budgets of Clement Augustus, where, on one occasion, by the side of 4716 thalers devoted *ad pias causas* figured 50,966 thalers for *Plaisiranschaffungen*, or various kinds of pleasures.

These pleasures, however, in many cases subserved indirectly a more useful purpose than that of merely contributing to the amusement of the illustrious prelate, whose post in the Church was nearly a sinecure, and the gay courtiers around him. Fortunately both for the art itself, and for the young musicians whose sole hope of encouragement and advancement rested in the private patron—long since supplanted by that new and still more powerful patron, the public—musical performances entered largely into the scheme of these *Plaisiranschaffungen.*

To Bonn, therefore, Beethoven's grandfather, with the energy and hopefulness of youth, a good voice, and musical capacity for stock-in-trade, made his way almost as a matter of course. Arrived there, his foot was soon on the first rung of the ladder; and after passing the customary year of probation, Ludvig found himself permanently installed among the court musicians, with an assured yearly income of four hundred gulden; already in a position, therefore, to face fortune with moderate equanimity. The successive steps by which, between the years 1732 and 1761, Ludvig rose from the post of ordinary musician to that of Capellmeister, and to a place third in the list of twenty-eight *Hommes de Chambre Honoraires* in the court, sufficiently testify to the favourable opinion of his abilities and character entertained by those about him. But for one dark shadow in his domestic life, the elder Ludvig's career might have been a happy as well as a successful one. This shadow was caused by an unfortunate propensity for drink manifested a few years after their marriage by his wife Josepha, and no doubt transmitted through her to their son Johann.

The career of Johann[1] Beethoven, father of the great composer, appears as a sombre interleaf between the unsullied page that preceded it and the glorious page that followed. It was marred rather by weakness and indecision of character than by actual badness. It began in mediocrity and ended in hopeless degeneracy and failure, his intemperate habits maintaining, as time went on, ever firmer hold of their victim. In 1767, possessing no other resources, apparently, than the miserable £30 a year his tenor voice enabled him to earn in the Electoral chapel, Johann plunged into matrimony, with consequences to himself and to others that might have been expected. He chose for wife a young widow, twelve years his junior, Marie Magdelena, daughter of the head-cook at the castle of Ehrenbreitstein; an honest, kindly woman, whose memory was cherished throughout his life by her son Ludvig with the tenderest affection.

Ludvig van Beethoven, the subject of this memoir, was baptized on the 17th December, 1770, an event commemorated a hundred years after by a tablet affixed to the house, No. 515, in the Bonngasse, where he was born. The date has been pretty generally quoted as that of the composer's birth, which, however, there is good reason for supposing occurred on the previous

[1] The name appears in early documents with various spellings—such as Biethofen, Biethoven, Bethoven, Betthoven and Bethof. It has been pointed out that whereas the dissipated Johann availed himself without stint of this latitude, his father, the elder Ludvig, an honourable man and citizen, was invariably consistent in the matter.

day. An elder brother, Ludvig Maria, born the year before, lived only six days. After Ludvig came Caspar Anton Carl (1774); Nickolaus Johann (1776); and August Franz Georg (1781). The latter died in early childhood, but Caspar and Johann lived to exercise an important and in some cases a sinister influence over the career of their distinguished brother. Besides a girl, who died four days after birth, another sister, Maria Margaretha Josepha, saw the light in 1786.

It would have fared hard with the little household from the outset but for the help contributed to the general expenses by Ludvig the elder. The worthy old Capellmeister continued the even course of his useful life, conducting at church, in the theatre, and at the Elector's private concerts, testing the qualifications of candidates for admission into the choir and orchestra, and supervising the musical arrangements at the court, with uniform industry and efficiency; a hale, bright-eyed man, the mainstay of the family while he lived, whose venerated figure often recurred to the composer's memory in after years.

All too soon the day arrived—before Ludvig was three years old—when that figure was removed from the scene. The grandfather died, and with his death ended the only happy days Ludvig can be said to have known in his childhood. While family sorrows thickened, and the pinch of poverty began to be felt in earnest, troubles of another kind, connected with that art which afterwards became the chief joy of his life, were in store for young Ludvig.

The signs of musical genius early manifested in

his boy set the needy Johann a-thinking. What direction his thoughts took, while he watched the small fingers struggling to pick out tunes upon the tinkling instrument that in those times supplied the place of pianoforte, may be inferred from his subsequent procedure. The pecuniary help long contributed by the most aged member of the family had ceased: was it not possible that this might now be replaced by judiciously exploiting the talents of the youngest? Naturally, perhaps, under the circumstances, his mind reverted to Handel's early successes, and to the still more recent successes of Mozart; and so, from that time forward, the process of "prodigy" forcing began in earnest. From his fourth year the hours not spent by Ludvig at the public school, where he received a second-rate education, were devoted remorselessly to an endless round of violin and clavier practice. Recreation and healthy exercise, such as usually fell to the lot of less gifted boys of his own age, were henceforth unknown to him. Tears and weariness, and, at length, something like hatred of the art he would otherwise have delighted in, were the natural consequence. Fortunately for Ludvig, Johann was sufficiently alive to his own interests, and sufficiently conscious of his own shortcomings as a teacher, to see the necessity of procuring further help; and with this view the services were called in of a tenor singer in the Bonn opera-house, named Pfeiffer, to whose hands the lad's musical education was transferred in 1779.

From all accounts this Pfeiffer seems to have been a helpful, capable, and withal kindly man; not altogether free, however, from the prodigy mania, nor unwilling to risk the young student's health, in his efforts to further the father's ambitious views. Pfeiffer, it is supposed, was lodging at that time in the same house as the Beethovens, and henceforth young Ludvig had two task-masters. The feeling of mingled gratitude and resentment with which in after life the composer looked back upon the severe training of these early years, is not without parallel in the lives of other men of genius, whose precocious powers raised hopes in others that cost them dear. No doubt Johann and Pfeiffer, in their eagerness for immediate results, pursued the forcing system—on some occasions at any rate—to the verge of inhumanity. We read of the pair coming home late at night from a drinking bout, and dragging the lad from his bed; of pianoforte practice prolonged till daybreak; of threats and punishments, and a general recklessness of treatment such as might easily have defeated its own object. Before passing unmitigated censure, it is only fair to look to results. They appear, at any rate, to have devoted immense pains in developing the powers of their pupil. At an age when other lads destined for a musical career were struggling with technical difficulties, young Beethoven was already sufficiently master of his art to begin to attempt the expression of what was in him; the period of preliminary discipline, inevitable for him as for all others, was already over. Judging too from the kindly feelings towards Pfeiffer, retained throughout his life by Beethoven himself, from a declaration he once made that "he had learned more from him than from anybody

B

else," from the fact that many years afterwards he sent money for the relief of his necessities through Simrock the music publisher, it is clear that the name of this, his first master, was not associated exclusively with memories of severity and unkindness.

To the pianoforte studies were added also lessons on the violin, and Ludvig's early initiation into the difficulties of the latter instrument proved still less to his taste: its necessity, however, will hardly be disputed. Meanwhile the lad was assisted by one Zambona in acquiring snatches of Latin, French, and Italian; and another indispensable part of his musical education was supplied by lessons on the organ from the court organist, Van den Eeden, an old friend of his late grandfather. Thus it will be seen that with all his faults and failings, Johann did honestly bestir himself to procure for his son such educational advantages as he was able to command by the help of family and professional connections; and that these advantages were considerable. In the following year (1781), Van den Eeden retired, and Christian Gottlob Neefe, succeeding to his post of organist to the court, undertook the further musical guidance of Van den Eeden's former pupil. This was an event of no small importance to Beethoven. Henceforth his organ studies brought him into daily contact with a musician of amiable disposition and undoubted ability, a conscientious teacher on old-fashioned lines, who enjoyed considerable influence in his day.

The relations between Neefe and his pupil continued for several years; not without some friction, but on the whole with friendly feeling on both sides, and with undoubted profit to Beethoven himself. This much was freely acknowledged by the latter, years after, in a letter addressed from Vienna to his old teacher. The differences which undoubtedly did occur from time to time to ruffle their intercourse are open to more than one explanation. Beethoven was always a "difficult" pupil to deal with; and the discipline of these early years must have been exasperating to one vaguely conscious of gifts destined hereafter to lead him whither his present Mentor would have neither the power nor probably the will to follow. Nevertheless, that he made rapid progress, is evident from the fact that Neefe, when compelled, with other members of the court band, to quit Bonn for the Elector's Palace at Munster, did not hesitate to appoint young Ludvig, then no more than eleven and a half years old, as his deputy at the chapel organ; a post of honour, but without emolument. In further explanation of the occasional friction that arose between them, is it uncharitable to suggest, while human nature remains what it is, that Neefe's admiration for his pupil's talents may have been accompanied with a vague misgiving lest some day they might prejudice his own position? If any such apprehensions really crossed his mind, he would have found some excuse for them in subsequent events; for the appointment enjoyed by Neefe was actually divided two years afterwards by order of Max Franz, the new Elector who succeeded on the death, in 1784, of Max Friedrich; and henceforth, out of a reduced salary of 350 florins, 150 florins went to the share of his pupil. Whatever may have been his feelings, Neefe was too worthy and too just a man to allow them to influence his acts; and he always showed himself ready to bear frank testimony to young Beethoven's abilities, whenever that testimony was likely to be useful to him. One instance of this genial appreciation is found in a letter from his pen published in *Cramer's Magazine*:—

"Louis Van Beethoven, a youth of eleven years, son of the aforesaid tenor, displays talent of considerable promise. He plays with power and finish, reads well at sight, and is able to execute the greater part of Sebastian Bach's *Wohl-temperirte Clavier*. Any one acquainted with this collection of preludes and fugues through all the keys (which might almost be called the *non plus ultra*) will know what this means. Herr Neefe has also given him, so far as other occupations will admit, some preliminary study of Thorough Bass. He is now exercising him in composition, and for his encouragement has had printed in Mannheim nine Variations on a March written by him for the pianoforte. This young genius deserves some assistance to enable him to travel. If he goes on as he has begun, he will certainly be a second Wolfgang Armadeus Mozart."

The variations above referred to were on a March of Dressler in C minor, to be found in Breitkopf and Härtel's edition of Beethoven's works. Originally the title-page contained one of those mystifications with which the world has since become familiar in questions pertaining to the age of prodigies. It is there stated that the piece was composed "par un jeune amateur, Ludvig von Beethoven, agé de dix ans".; whereas the "young amateur" was already twelve years old.

Among Beethoven's earliest compositions were three Sonatas for the pianoforte, published in 1781 and 1782, and dedicated to the Elector Max Friedrich in terms of flattery and servility—no doubt supplied to him by others—characteristic of such productions in that age of patronage. We also hear of a Funeral Cantata, which has unfortunately been lost. This was written and performed in memory of Mr. Cressener, for some years the English *chargé d'affaires* at Bonn, a gentleman of cultivated tastes, who appears to have quickly discerned the phenomonal character of the boy's genius, and whose appreciation took the practical and welcome form of a gift of four hundred florins.

There is no record of public appearances at this time, nor indeed until many years afterwards. The nearest approach to the kind of musical baby-farming so familiar in our modern concert-rooms was a tour in Holland, supposed to have been made by Ludvig and his mother in the winter of 1781. Some such step may well have been unavoidable, considering the desperate straits into which the family had fallen since the grandfather's death. The youthful *virtuoso*, probably, reaped a two-fold advantage from this journey, in presents received from well-to-do persons whose houses he visited, and in the increased self-confidence he cannot have failed to acquire by thus continually playing before strangers.

In 1783 the Elector was much occupied with a project for establishing at Bonn a National Opera Company, in imitation of that at Vienna. He engaged, with this view, a body of vocalists, named after their manageress, "The Grossmann Company," and

Neefe, who had formerly been connected with the troupe, was appointed director. The event brought with it yet another advancement for Ludvig. There can be no stronger proof of the high estimation in which his talents were already held by those above him than the fact that at the age of twelve years and four months young Beethoven was formally installed as cembalist in the orchestra. The duties attached to this post were by no means light, and required both skill and knowledge for their proper fulfilment. When presiding at the piano during rehearsals, the cembalist was expected to play all accompaniments from score; and, seeing that the performances given between 1783 and 1785 included operas by Gluck, Salieri, Sarti, Paisiello, and many others, this connection with the theatre must have afforded him important opportunities for self-improvement. He had to be contented, however, with the honour of the appointment, as no remuneration was at first attached to it.

The death, in April 1784, of the Elector Max Friedrich brought many changes and some disappointments; among them the abandonment of the scheme for National Opera-house, and the consequent dismissal of the theatrical company. Once released from the burden of duties which had weighed very heavily upon him, Neefe returned to the organ, and no longer needed a deputy. For a time, therefore, Ludvig's connection with the court chapel ceased, and his engagements as organist dwindled down to the playing of early morning mass in the Minorite church. The pay, if any, received for this service must have been a mere pittance; and though Ludvig managed to earn a little money by teaching—always an irksome and hateful task for him —that year was no doubt remembered as one of the darkest for the never very prosperous Beethoven family; especially when it is considered that to money perplexities were added others arising from the father's ever-increasing intemperance.

But in June, when the new Elector began to reorganize his establishment, the outlook again brightened. Among the changes in his musical arrangements was one which must have proved more palatable to young Beethoven than to his master; for it was then that the division of duties and emoluments took place, as already related, according to which Ludvig became henceforth organist jointly with Neefe. There had been, indeed, some idea of dismissing Neefe altogether, and installing Beethoven in his place. In the list issued by Max Franz in 1784 of the various members of his band and their respective salaries, Ludvig figures for the first time as "second organist," with a yearly stipend of about fifteen pounds, while that of his father was about thirty pounds.

An era of increased musical activity commenced with the reign of Max Franz, a prince who surpassed even his predecessors in the splendour of his court, and the discriminate exercise of patronage in all matters connected with art. No doubt young Beethoven's ardent and sensitive temperament was favourably influenced by the prevailing enthusiasm. That he was in better spirits may be inferred from the little practical joke recorded against him during the Holy Week of 1785, brief-mention of which, familiar as it is, demands a place here. At the services held in Passion Week organ-playing was prohibited ; but it was customary for the accompanist to improvise short interludes upon the pianoforte between the selected phrases from the Lamentations of Jeremiah sung upon such occasions. A singer in the Electoral chapel named Heller, over-confident in his own powers, made a bet with Beethoven that the latter would be unable to confuse his ear in the course of these voluntaries by any legitimate modulation, however foreign to the original key. This challenge resulted in a signal victory of composer over vocalist. Whether or not Beethoven's harmonies were of a kind that would be called "license" in the present day—and probably by a less tolerant name by the more strait-laced musicians of those times—he succeeded to his heart's content in throwing the soloist out of tune and out of temper. The singer's discomfiture gave rise to an insignificant professional squabble, in which even Max Franz himself was asked to interfere.

The year 1786 was uneventful in an artistic, or at any rate in an artistically productive sense; but in those lively times at Bonn, when each day brought some new excitement, some court festivity, notable arrival, long rehearsal, or important performance, the young musician cannot have been idle. The year that followed, on the other hand, was destined to be an important landmark in his career. Amid the life and bustle of the little court in Bonn, it is easy to imagine with what fervent longing the thoughts of a young and ambitious composer must have turned towards that still more important centre of musical life—Vienna. How long a project of visiting the brilliant capital had been dimly shaping itself in his mind, or by what means the apparently unsurmountable difficulties to its realization were eventually overcome, there is no evidence to show. The contrast between the gay scenes amid which his professional duties were performed and his meagre home—where, since the birth of a sister, Marie Margaretha Josepha, in 1786, the pressure of poverty weighed ever more heavily—must have been a source of daily and hourly pain to him. Such information as the world possesses of his resources, and of the financial condition of the family at that time, by no means favours the suggestion that he was able out of his salary and some few poorly paid music-lessons to save sufficient money to cover the expenses of such a journey. Whatever the quarter from which help for this purpose was obtained, to Vienna he went, in the year ever memorable for him, 1787.

Shortly after Beethoven's arrival at that capital, yet another of his cherished dreams was realized—he was introduced to Mozart. Viewed in the light of after events, this meeting between the composer with whose fame the whole musical world was then ringing, and the young "musician of the future," destined hereafter to eclipse, by the daring and grandeur of his achievements, even the great maestro himself, has a peculiar interest. The interview occurred at a musical gathering, and took a course, in the first instance, that might easily have been foreseen. As may be supposed, Mozart in his time had had no small experience of "boy-wonders," and what he had hitherto seen of the phenomenon was not likely to cause him to be over-sanguine in the present case. When Beethoven, therefore, commenced with what he suspected to be the regulation show-piece, the master contented himself with a few words of conventional praise. But afterwards, when the new player asked to be allowed to extemporize upon a given theme, and, warming to his subject, gave full rein to his imagination, Mozart quickly changed his tone, and expressed admiration in sufficiently generous terms. Passing quietly into the adjoining room, he said to the friends about him—"Pay heed to this youth; one of these days he will make a noise in the world." In spite of his many pre-occupations, artistic and social, Mozart found time to give Beethoven a few lessons; but these do not appear to have left a very favourable impression upon the mind of the critical scholar.

Another event, long remembered in connection with these halcyon days—to be cut short, all too soon, by bad news from home—was his introduction to the Emperor Francis Joseph; the precise date of which has not been conclusively fixed. We know that in July Beethoven had already returned to Bonn; and, as Thayer with his customary minuteness points out, seeing that the emperor accompanied Catherine of Russia on a visit to the Crimea between April 11th and June 30th of the same year, the meeting must have taken place either before the first or after the second of these dates.

The summer, which had commenced so hopefully, and had brought with it so much unwonted excitement for Ludvig, was suddenly darkened by a grave domestic sorrow. News reached him from home that his mother was dying of consumption, and an immediate return to Bonn became necessary. The journey was not accomplished without difficulty; and it will be seen from the following letter addressed to Dr. Von Schaden of Augsburg, that he was compelled to borrow a sum equivalent to about £3 to help him on his way:—

"*Bonn*, 1787. *Autumn*.

"ESTEEMED AND WORTHY FRIEND,

"What you must think of me I can easily imagine; that you have good reason not to think favourably of me I am unable to deny; but I will not excuse myself until I have explained my reasons for hoping that you will accept my apologies.

"I must tell you in the first place that since I left Augsburg, my cheerfulness and with it my health began to fail me. The nearer I came to my native city, the more letters did I receive from my father, urging me to travel as fast as possible, in view of my mother's precarious state of health; so, though far from well myself, I hurried on as fast as possible. The longing to see my dying mother once again helped me to overcome all obstacles. I found my mother still alive, but in a terrible condition. Her malady was consumption, and about seven weeks ago after much intense suffering she died. So good, so amiable a mother as she was! My best friend! Ah, who was happier than I, so long as I was able to utter the sweet name of mother, and to know that I was heard! And to whom can I now say it? To the silent images of her that my imagination conjures up for me? Since my return here I have had but few happy hours. I have suffered from asthma the whole time, and fear that it will eventually result in consumption. In addition to this, I am a prey to melancholy, for me an evil as serious as illness itself. Imagine yourself in my place, and I may then hope to obtain your forgiveness. With regard to your extreme goodness and kindness in lending me three Carolines in Augsburg, I am compelled to ask your indulgence for a little longer. My journey has been very expensive, and here I have not the slightest hope of earning anything. Fate does not favour me here in Bonn.

"Pardon me for troubling you with this long statement about myself. It was necessary to make it in my own extenuation.

"Do not, I pray you, withdraw from me your much-prized friendship. There is nothing I so ardently wish as to make myself worthy of it.

"I am, with all esteem,
"Your most obedient servant and friend,
"L. V. BEETHOVEN,
"*Cologne Court Organist.*"

"*To* MONSIEUR DE SCHADEN,
"*Counsellor at Augsburg.*"

His mother died on the 17th July. During her last illness she was tended by her old friend Franz Ries with an affectionate devotion that Beethoven never forgot. In November his little sister Margaretha also passed away; and thus the year 1787 ended in sorrow and despondency.

One result of these changes was to burden the young

musician with new responsibilities, and after the bustle and excitement of his Vienna trip, and the reaction following upon its mournful termination, he must have resumed his daily round of duties in the little town of Bonn with a heavy heart. The stipend of about £30 a year, earned by his father as one of the musicians of the court, represented that worthy's sole contribution towards general expenses; and seeing that Johann's voice was already considerably impaired by long-continued excesses, the sum, small as it was, probably represented not an unfair equivalent for his services according to the scale of remuneration in those days. Young Ludvig added a little by his music teaching, and the absolute necessity of increased exertions in that direction, if the household was to be kept together, soon became evident. For the sake of those at home higher ambitions had to be postponed, and hour after hour snatched from composition and the pursuits he loved, to help the halting steps of learners in various stages of inefficiency. The days of guinea music-lessons were not then within measurable distance; but however small may have been the pay, rich compensation for his self-sacrifice was in store for Ludvig; for it was while engaged in this weary and uncongenial occupation that he formed the most valuable and lasting friendship of his life.

Among the families with which Beethoven was brought into contact was one occupying a high social position at Bonn, named Von Breuning. He first made their acquaintance as music-master to the youngest son Lenz and his sister; but soon this acquaintance ripened into an intimacy, the benign influence of which over Beethoven's future can hardly be over-estimated. This charming home, brightened by genuine enthusiasm for all matters pertaining to art and literature, and made doubly fair by refinement of manners and mutual affection, must have been a veritable haven of rest for the young and struggling musician. The circle consisted of Madame Von Breuning, a woman of cultivated tastes and kindly heart, widow of a councillor of State who had perished in a fire at the Electoral Palace; her three sons, Christoph, Stephan, and Lenz; and their sister Eleanore. There was also living at the house, Madame Von Breuning's brother, the Canon Abraham V. Keferich, who superintended the children's education. Fresh hopes, new and cheerier views of life and its possibilities, came to Beethoven amid these surroundings, and whatever taste for general culture he possessed in addition to his musical gifts, may fairly be attributed to this happy period. The young men wrote poetry, and studied the ancient classical writers in the original under their uncle's guidance. Ludvig did not, apparently, go so far as this; but the *Odyssey* in Voss's translation was a constant source of delight to him, and he read with avidity not only the works of Lessing and Klopstock and Gleim, and the early productions of Goethe, but also certain German versions of Shakespere and Milton and Sterne—desultory studies which but imperfectly supplied the place of that general education his father, eager and exacting as he was in the matter of musical training, had so culpably neglected.

Valuable above all was the friendship extended to

him by Madame Von Breuning. In her Beethoven at last found the encouragement and moral support he had so long needed. The affection which sprung up between the two, indeed, resembled that of mother and son. Madame Von Breuning thoroughly appreciated both his genius and his strong, sterling character. Even when Beethoven was in one of his least tractable moods, a word from her would suffice to restore the lost balance, and it was to her he would turn as a matter of course in the first instance for sympathy and counsel. His aversion to teaching has already been referred to; and here again, when he was inclined to be more than unusually restive, Madame Breuning would interfere with the most salutary results. "Beethoven has had a 'raptus'" was her favourite expression in explanation of any exceptional eccentricity on the part of the young musician; and this word came to be a standing joke between them for years afterwards. In those days the need of such sympathy was often felt by Ludvig, for his life, in spite of its more congenial surroundings, was still far from a happy one. Troubles at home increased as Johann's intemperate habits became ever more confirmed and were followed by their inevitable consequences. Thanks to the forbearance of the Elector, his salary still continued, but the services rendered by him in exchange had for some time past been merely nominal. We hear of an escapade on one occasion with the police, in which Stephan Breuning had to come to the rescue. In short, it became evident that the unfortunate tenor was no longer fit to be intrusted with the administration of the slender resources of the household, or with the fate of his children; and by an arrangement concluded, with the Elector's sanction, in November 1789, part of Johann's salary was henceforth paid over to Ludvig, who thus, under the age of nineteen, found himself saddled with the cares and responsibilities of a family.

At about this time Count Waldstein, an enthusiastic and cultivated amateur of music, was staying at Bonn, previous to his admission into the Teutonic order of which Max Franz was Grand-Master. In this accomplished nobleman Beethoven found another valuable friend, who not only brightened existence by his genial companionship, but found opportunities to assist him in other ways. His services were as generous as they were delicately rendered. He presented him with a piano; he caused money to be conveyed to him under the guise of allowances from the Elector, and spared neither time, trouble, nor influence in his efforts to promote the advancement of his *protégé*. His name will be handed down to generations, by whom, probably, it would otherwise be forgotten, in association with the famous Sonata, Op. 53, which some fifteen years later Beethoven dedicated to him in token of his gratitude. Scarcely less valuable than pecuniary aid was the artistic stimulus obtained by the musician during this intercourse with his warm-hearted and sympathetic admirer. Waldstein would often pay a visit to his shabby room, and while Ludvig, seated at the piano, played and improvised under conditions likely to display his powers at their best, the aristocratic amateur would throw in words of encouragement and advice. For on such occasions Waldstein often played the part of more than a mere listener. Towards the end of 1790, Beethoven undertook to compose music for a brilliant *bal masqué*, which Waldstein intended to give early in the following year. The plan bore fruit in the *Ritter Ballet.* This was duly performed, and for some time the authorship of the music was attributed to Waldstein himself; the truth being that Waldstein made suggestions and Beethoven carried them into effect.

Among those who always found a friendly welcome at the Breunings' were Franz Ries, and Beethoven's old chum and future biographer, Wegeler—attracted there, we may suppose, by considerations not altogether unconnected with the daughter of the house—Eleanore—whom he afterwards married. How frequently Ludvig's extempore powers were brought into requisition during those happy social evenings can be easily imagined. All sorts of fanciful subjects were suggested to him. He would invent on the spur of the moment little tone-pictures of various persons of their acquaintance, and on one occasion Ries on his violoncello and Beethoven on the piano gave a joint improvisation. Often in the days to come, when Beethoven found himself the central figure of attraction in the courtly drawing-rooms of Vienna, must his thoughts have wandered back regretfully to these peaceful evenings that passed all too quickly in harmless merriment, music, art-talk, and the purest social enjoyment.

The scheme for establishing a national theatre was revived by the new Elector, but Beethoven no longer acted as cembalist. For four years he played the violin in the orchestra—sometimes by the side of Stephan Breuning, himself a capable amateur—and thus had an opportunity of further acquainting himself with the characteristics of stringed instruments. His connection with the court band also brought with it many a little festive incident to relieve the monotony of professional duties. One such was associated with a specially happy time, and made a lasting impression upon him.

When the Elector visited Mergentheim in his capacity of Grand-Master of the Teutonic Order at Bonn, an excursion by water to accompany him was undertaken by the chief members of the orchestra. Two vessels were chartered, and the occasion served as an excuse for a sort of masquerade, into the spirit of which the whole company threw themselves with the utmost enthusiasm. The first comedian, Lux, was elected king; and a distribution of other offices and state dignities followed in due course. To Beethoven was allotted, in the first instance, the post of king's scullion, and in this he acquitted himself to the general satisfaction. He was afterwards promoted; and Wegeler mentions having found among Beethoven's papers, a formidable document, sealed, tied, and stamped with pitch, which represented the letters patent.

Amid song and laughter and good-natured fooling the merry crew floated up the river through some of the most beautiful parts of Rhineland. The charm of the scenery, viewed at its best from the boats as they glided leisurely along, the sunlit hills, the pure air, the absence of constraint—all combined to make this holiday a memorable one for the light-hearted youths who took part in it. The event has since been celebrated in song by the poet Kauffman, and Beethoven used to refer to it as "a fruitful source of beautiful images."

Their journey was broken at Aschaffenburg, where lived the Abbé Sterkel, the eminent pianist and prolific composer; and a plan was formed by some of the holiday-makers to pay him a visit. Thanks to the good offices of Ries and Simrock, Beethoven was included among the party, and introduced to the distinguished amateur, whose name, of course, had long been familiar to him. They met with a kindly and hospitable reception; the Abbé little dreaming that the part he played as host that day would hereafter be recorded in history. He gave them, by general request, a specimen of the refined and graceful style of playing for which he was famous. Beethoven was then persuaded by his companions—not without difficulty and the aid of a little diplomacy—to seat himself at the piano. A sly remark in connection with his recently published twenty-four variations on Righini's *Venni Amore*, coupled with a declaration from the Abbé that in his belief not even the composer himself would be able to cope with their difficulties, served its purpose. For not only did the composer surmount those difficulties, but he invented, on the spur of the moment, others still more formidable, adopting for the nonce, either in a freak or in unconscious imitation, something of the refinement and elegance of the Abbé's playing. Beethoven's performance on that occasion made a deep impression upon all who heard it, and his visit to the learned Abbé was a decided success. So far as is known, the two never came together again.

On their arrival at Mergentheim the company gave a series of immensely successful representations, and they remained there about a month. The effect produced upon his hearers by Beethoven's playing at that time —rough as it is said to have been in technique—may be seen from an interesting description of it furnished by Carl Ludwig Junker, chaplain to Prince Hohenlohe. His notice, which appeared in a contemporary paper, also gives pleasant testimony to the high personal regard entertained towards the young composer by those who were brought into contact with him.

"I have also heard," says Junker, "one of the greatest pianists—the dear good Beethoven, some of whose compositions, written at eleven years of age, appeared in 1783. He declined to play at a public concert, perhaps because he did not like to perform on one of Spath's pianos, being accustomed at Bonn to Stein's instruments. But what was infinitely better, I heard him improvise; in fact I was myself asked to give him a theme. The greatness of this gentle and amiable man as a *virtuoso* may, I think, be estimated by the inexhaustible wealth of his imagination, the skill of his execution, and the thorough originality of his expression. I did not find him deficient in any of the attributes of a great artist. I have frequently heard Vogler play the piano for hour after hour (of his organ playing I express no opinion, for I never heard it), and always admired his extraordinary dexterity; but Beethoven, in addition to his fluent execution, is more telling, suggestive, expressive—in a word, he touches the heart, and he is as good in *adagio* as in *allegro*. The clever artists of this band are his admirers one and all, and listen intently when he plays. But he is modest and quite unassuming. Yet he acknowledged that on the tours which he undertook by order of the Elector, he rarely found in the most celebrated pianists what he had thought himself justified in expecting. His playing differs also so widely from the ordinary mode, that he appears to have obtained his present high profession by altogether original means."

As will be seen hereafter, it was the magic of the Rhenish musician's pianoforte playing, above all his wonderful gift of improvisation, that in the first instance roused the enthusiasm of Viennese amateurs. Haydn, we are told, went so far as to prophesy greater things of Beethoven as a *virtuoso* than as a composer.

With reference to the comparison above quoted between the playing of Vogler and of Beethoven, it should be remembered that the former—a native of Salzburg, as was also the other musical Abbé met by Beethoven at Aschaffenburg—was one of the most remarkable composers, theorists, and organists of his age.

The Elector's band returned to Bonn in time for Christmas, and resumed their work-a-day life. This continued to be brightened for Beethoven by his intercourse with the Breuning family, in whose house a new attraction presently appeared in the young and charming Jeannette d'Honrath, a friend and occasional visitor of Eleanore von Breuning. Beethoven soon lost his heart to the Cologne beauty, who during her stay seems to have enlivened the time by flirting indiscriminately with both Stephan and Ludvig, though the wounds she inflicted were neither very deep nor lasting—fortunately as it afterwards turned out; for her affections had already been bestowed upon a young Austrian officer, whom she ultimately married. The charms of another of the Breunings' visitors, the beautiful Miss Westerholz, also brought him under the thraldom of a hopeless affection, and for a season made him duly miserable. This was the *Wertherliebe* about which his friend Bernhard Romberg used to tell anecdotes twenty years later.

Beethoven never married; but his love affairs throughout life were very numerous. Such tender episodes varied in degrees of seriousness from the passing fancy to those passionate attachments that alternately raised him to the seventh heaven of happiness, and plunged him into the depths of despair. The very fact that his intense longing for a home and for female companionship was never satisfied, that his affections never passed beyond the early stage during which life for him was surrounded by a glamour of romance and poetry and feverish hopes never to be realized, exercised a powerful and inevitable influence over the artistic side of his nature, and gave to his music in many cases a special character. Had he been fortunate enough, like Mozart, to find a Constance, the effect of this happier life would no doubt have made itself felt in his works; might even have improved them; but those works could never have been exactly what they were. "So long at any rate as I knew him," says Wegeler, "Beethoven was never without a love, and he achieved conquest where many an Adonis had failed before him." Similar testimony has been given by his friends, Breuning, Ries, and Romberg; and Wegeler adds the remark, that the objects of Beethoven's affections were nearly always ladies occupying a position in life superior to his own—a fact that goes far towards explaining his many disappointments.

As far as his interesting young pupil Eleanore von Breuning was concerned, the susceptible young musician appears to have escaped scot free. She was indeed engaged, or on the eve of engagement, to his friend Wegeler, whose wife she afterwards became. Between her and Ludvig a sincere affection existed, but it was that of brother and sister; an affection which, with but one interruption, was preserved by both to the end of their lives. This interruption was caused by a difference that arose between them, for some unascertained reason, shortly before Beethoven's departure from Bonn. Among the few relics of youthful days, discovered among his papers, was the following greeting, accompanied with a wreath of flowers, sent him by Eleanore on his twentieth birthday—

"ZU B.'S GEBURTSTAG VON SEINER SCHÜLERIN.

"Glück und langes Leben
Wünsch' ich heute Dir,
Aber auch daneben
Wünsch' ich etwas mir!

"Mir in Rücksicht Deiner,
Wünsch' ich Deine Huld.
Dir in Rücksicht meiner,
Nachsicht und Geduld!
"Von Ihrer Freundin und Schülerin,
"LORCHEN V. BREUNING."

An air of innocent romance also surrounds Ludvig's frequent visits to the 'Zehrgarten,' a tavern greatly favoured at that time by the professors and students of the university, and by others connected with literary and scientific pursuits. The house of entertainment offered other inducements to Ludvig besides those of good-fellowship and intellectual converse; for here was to be found the pretty Babette Koch, daughter of the proprietress. Babette was a girl of considerable attainments, and a just estimate of the position she occupied in the Bonn community is scarcely to be formed by reference to modern social prejudices. That she was good as well as pretty, may be safely inferred from the fact that she was able to reckon among her friends Eleanore von Breuning. She afterwards undertook the post of governess to the children of Count Belderbusch, and ended by marrying the father of her charges, and thus becoming a countess. In a letter written to Eleanore by Beethoven, a year after he had settled in Vienna, it will be seen that he had by no means forgotten the beauty of Bonn.

Meanwhile, Beethoven's two brothers, who figure with such unfortunate prominency in the story of his later life, had chosen their vocations; Carl studying music, while Johann served an apprenticeship under the court apothecary.

In 1790, Haydn, accompanied by Saloman, had passed through Bonn on his way to London. Again in 1792 the music-loving inhabitants were stirred to enthusiasm by the presence among them, on his return journey, of the famous Austrian composer. The visit was a memorable one for Beethoven; and certain incidents connected with it bore an important part in the shaping of his future career. At Godesberg a dinner was given to the traveller by the Elector's band; and on that occasion Ludvig had an opportunity of submitting to him an unpublished cantata, now known to have been that composed on the death of the Emperor Joseph II. Until lately the work in question was supposed to have been lost. It is written for solo, chorus and orchestra, and was published for the first time in Breitkopt and Härtel's last volume. Haydn was warm in his praises of the work, and encouraged the young musician to continue his studies. Though little is known of the conversation that ensued between the two, it is not unreasonable to connect this episode with events that followed closely upon it.

The eyes of the Elector Max Franz seem at last to have been opened to the fact, that among the musicians at his court was one, at least, who was endowed with exceptional qualities. He had witnessed the steady advances in his art made by the young Beethoven; the ready efficiency he showed in every new post that was assigned to him; the admiration he commanded among his musical associates. The high esteem in which the young musician was held by Neefe, the Breunings, and Count Waldstein cannot have been unknown to him. No doubt, too, Haydn's favourable verdict upon his work was not long in reaching the Elector's ears, and the impression thus produced upon his mind was probably strengthened by many a good word from Waldstein, ever on the alert to promote the advancement of his friend and *protégé*. The outcome of all this was a change of the happiest kind in Beethoven's prospects, bringing to a close the first stage of his artistic career.

For some time past fate had been drawing Beethoven with invisible threads in the direction of Vienna. His dream of returning once more to that capital, of making there a prolonged sojourn, of receiving lessons from Haydn, of obtaining admission into the charmed circle of a society that had become famous throughout Europe for intellectual culture and liberal patronage, had seemed doubly hopeless since the death of his mother, and in view of the additional responsibilities thrown upon his shoulders by his father's incapacity. But this dream was now to be realized. The money difficulty, which alone stood in the way, was removed by a pension from the Elector, and by other small sums given him to start with, either by the Elector or some one else.

Some sadness must have mingled with Beethoven's natural exultation, at the prospect of severance from the home of his childhood, where, in spite of trials and privations, he had passed many a happy hour, and formed many a lifelong friendship. But this severance could not have been long delayed. Soon revolutionary events changed all the old conditions, and brought to an end any hopes he might have entertained of further advancement in his native place. When Beethoven left Bonn, if he did not "burn his ships," it may be said, at any rate, that they were burnt for him. An unexpected turn of Fortune's wheel was in store also for many of those he left behind; for his noble patron among the number. Political troubles filled the air; within a short time Elector, courtiers, musicians, and actors were all to be swept away by the tide of the French Revolution; and when, in October, the French troops threatened the Rhine, all the Rhenish towns, including Cologne itself, were thrown into a state of panic; most members of the upper classes packed up their valuables and took flight; and following the general example, the Elector Max Franz withdrew to Mergentheim.

The many hands that were outstretched in farewell greeting as soon as Ludvig's impending departure became known, the Godspeeds and affectionate congratulations showered upon him from all sides, sufficiently testify to the young musician's popularity with his companions. Waldstein's parting words have come to possess almost historic interest—

"DEAR BEETHOVEN,

"You are now going to Vienna in fulfilment of your wish so long frustrated. The genius of Mozart still weeps and mourns the death of his pupil. He found an asylum but no employment in the inexhaustible genius of Haydn. Through him he now wishes to be united to some one else. Receive, through unbroken industry, from the hands of Haydn the spirit of Mozart.

"Your true friend,

"WALDSTEIN."

"*Bonn, 29th October*, 1792."

Needless to say that the Breunings, Wegeler, Franz Ries, Neefe, Reicha, Degenhart, and many others, were not behindhand in good wishes. Their names, with a few valedictory words from each, were inscribed, together with the above letter from Waldstein, in an album which Beethoven preserved as one of the most precious mementoes of his youthful days, and which is still in existence. Early in November he set forth on his journey, and the old familiar streets of his native Bonn knew him no more.

Beethoven was now approaching his twenty-second year. A comparison has often been instituted between the paucity of his written compositions up to that time and the phenomenal productiveness shown during their youth by many other great musicians. Especially will such a comparison suggest itself in view of the vast amount of work achieved by Mozart during a similar period.

Before the age of twenty-three, the latter had already established his fame as a prolific writer of symphonies, of operas, of cantatas, and masses; including juvenile productions, he was able to point to some three hundred works from his pen. By the side of this astonishing record, that of Beethoven, as far as quantity is concerned, is altogether insignificant—the single orchestral piece belonging to the Bonn period being the *Ritter Ballet.* But of the activity of Beethoven's inventive powers during youth we should have ample proof—if proof were needed—in the extraordinary merit and fluency of his extempore playing. A partial explanation of the sort of reserve which seems hitherto to have held him back, when it came to putting pen to paper, may perhaps be found in his known methods of composition, and in his favourite habit of leaving notions to lie fallow —developing, altering, and slowly perfecting them with a patient self-criticism, of which some very interesting examples appear in the celebrated "Sketch-Books" given to the world by Mr. Nottebohm.

During those years of comparative unproductiveness he had no doubt written much and destroyed much, and formed many projects the world knew nothing of. A letter addressed to Schiller's sister Charlotte by a friend from Bonn, in January 1793, encloses for her opinion a setting of the *Feuer-farbe*, and then goes on to say—"It is the work of a young man of this place, whose musical talent has been universally recognized, and whom the Elector has now sent to Vienna, to Haydn. He means to set to work upon Schiller's *Freude*, verse by verse. I expect something perfect; for, so far as I know him, he is all for the grand and elevated. Haydn states he intends to set him to grand operas, as he himself will shortly have to leave off composing. He does not usually devote himself to trifles like the enclosed, which was composed at the request of a lady." In a letter to Eleanore von Breuning, written not later than the spring of 1794, Beethoven excuses himself for not sending the "long-promised sonata." Thayer interprets this to refer to a certain sonata he had played at her house in the old Bonn days, and promised to copy out from the rough sketch still in his possession. Casual mention also is made, in a Vienna musical paper of 1796, of "several beautiful sonatas" by the new virtuoso, the existence of which in MS. appears to have been well known while he was pursuing his studies under Haydn and Albrechtsberger.

Unobtrusively and without flourish of trumpets the future king of symphonists made his entry into that capital which was henceforth to be the scene of his struggles and triumphs; selecting for his first lodging a garret—presently exchanged for a room on the ground-floor—at a printer's house in the Alservorstadt, there to commence a term of student-life which lasted about three years. In accordance with arrangements made beforehand, his lessons under Haydn commenced almost immediately, and were received at the master's house. These included the usual curriculum of "strict counterpoint" according to Fux, whose *Gradus ad Parnassum* was used. The Elector's allowance—not a very large one, and not long continued—with the addition, perhaps, of further help from other quarters, enabled him to purchase a few articles required for his personal comfort, and student's paraphernalia. Untidy as Beethoven often was from a housewife's point of view, he had acquired at least some methodical habits, and he kept periodical record not only of musical ideas, but of daily expenses. From one of these memoranda we learn that during his first month in Vienna he invested in stick, wig, boots, shoes, overcoat, seal, desk, and the hire of a piano.

It is interesting to think that during the time Beethoven was working modestly in Vienna, under the guidance of two famous masters, his name as a composer had already come to be known and honoured among at least one little musical *coterie* in an English provincial town. When most of the well-to-do inhabitants of Bonn were hastily packing up their belongings and preparing for flight, a certain Abbé Dobbeler, having occasion to go to Hamburg, offered his escort thus far to an old English lady who was on her way home. This was the Hon. Mrs. Bowater, a cosmopolitan traveller, of cultivated musical taste, who had lived on the Continent for many years. Business afterwards called the Abbé to England, whence the two went together, and eventually they took up their residence at Leicester. As the ecclesiastic was an excellent violinist, music became one of the favourite consolations of his exile. A friend of both living in the same town relates how, on a rainy day, he would often receive from the Abbé some such missive as the following—"As the day is good for nothing but dinner and music, Mrs. Bowater hopes for your company at four, and a quartet in the evening." The interest of these cosy meetings consists in the fact that among the music played, and always with the greatest enthusiasm, was a trio, brought over from Bonn by Abbé Dobbeler, the work of a then new composer—Ludvig van Beethoven. In London also, it should be added, the three pianoforte trios, Op. 1—composed 1791-92, and dedicated to Prince Lichnowsky—were greeted with acclamation by Cramer, Watts the tenor, and other musicians.

In Vienna, as in England a hundred years ago, the pursuit of music in any serious or elevated sense was restricted to the aristocratic and privileged classes; but in those circles it had reached a degree of dignity, refinement, and importance which would have been impossible, during those times at any rate, under other conditions. The conditions, it is true, were those of patronage, and patronage in its most unqualified and undisguised form Representatives of noble houses had their own private orchestras and quartets; a fashion, and in many cases a sincere love, for chamber music stimulated the industry of composers in that pure and beautiful form of art, which then reached its highest point of development, and has since for the most part been strangely neglected. Among the great families he visited, Beethoven found many true friends, well able to appreciate his character and his genius; but that his proud spirit sometimes rebelled against this patronage, and would have been happier to follow an artistic career under those more independent conditions now possible to great composers and *virtuosi*, is sufficiently proved by his distaste for playing before company, and by his occasional outbreaks of downright rudeness when asked to do so.

Wegeler has told us that all gaiety forsook Beethoven whenever he was asked to play in society. "He would come to me moody and depressed, and would say they forced him to play till the blood tingled to the very tips of his fingers. Gradually I would draw him into a friendly conversation, and try to quiet him and divert his thoughts. This accomplished, I let the conversation drop. I went to my desk, and if Beethoven wanted to say anything more he was obliged to take a chair just in front of the pianoforte. Soon, without turning round, he would strike one or two chords of an undecided character, and out of these the most beautiful melodies gradually arose. I did not venture to make any remark about his playing, or only referred to it casually." This aversion to public display always remained, and was often the cause of unpleasantness with his best friends.

Thayer has given a list of some of the principal houses at which Beethoven attended private musical entertainments, and was on a more or less friendly footing during his second winter in Vienna. Among such were the houses of Princes Lobkowitz, Lichnowsky, Lichtenstein, Esterhazy, Schwarzenberg, Auersperg, Kinsky, Trautmannsdorff, and Eisendorf; of the Counts Appony Browne, Ballassa, Franz and Johann Esterhazy, Czernin, Erdödy, Fries, Strassaldo, and Zichy; the Countesses Hatzfeld and Thun; Barons Lang, Partenstein, van Swieten, and von Rees; Counsellors Meyer, Greiner, Paradies; Fräulein Martinez; the banker Henikstein, and others—an extensive visiting list for which the young student was indebted to introductions given him by his influential friend Waldstein, and to the connections which grew out of them. In the course of this round of musical *réunions* Beethoven was naturally brought into contact with many of the best-known pianists of the time, and had an opportunity of confirming his opinion, formerly confided to Junker, that closer acquaintance with the performances of famous *virtuosi* often brought with it a measure of disappointment.

He had not been more than a month at Vienna before news reached him from home of the death of his father. This event rendered necessary immediate steps for the protection of his two younger brothers, whose sole natural guardian he now became. As the pension of one hundred thalers, upon which they had depended for support, now ceased, Beethoven petitioned the Elector for its continuance. His request was granted, and Ries undertook to receive and administer the money. This assistance, however, together with the allowance granted to Beethoven himself, ceased altogether after 1794, when the Elector and his court were forced to fly from Bonn before the insurgent troops.

The feeling of disillusion already experienced by Beethoven when brought to close quarters with certain celebrities of the day, was repeated in the case of Haydn as soon as he became his regular pupil. Perfect sympathy between two such natures was indeed scarcely to be expected: one self-willed, rough in manner, and impatient of etiquette; the other well-trained in the school of patronage, ceremonious, and deferent to his social superiors—one full of fire, and daring, and premonitions of future greatness; the other living and working industriously within that calmer sphere of art in which he reigned supreme, a thorough master of his resources, with settled powers and settled convictions. What were the exact relations at this time between master and pupil, and how far some of the disparaging remarks recorded of Beethoven may be attributed to momentary fits of anger, are questions that have never been clearly answered. Those relations, however, are well known to have been not altogether satisfactory, and although there were no open hostilities, they lived on terms of intimacy, if not of very warm friendship. The minute diary kept by

Beethoven of current expenses, shows that he occasionally paid for his master's coffee and chocolate.

Besides being disappointed with his hero, Beethoven considered he had specific cause for dissatisfaction at the perfunctory manner in which Haydn's duties towards him as a teacher were fulfilled; and a circumstance presently occurred which went far to confirm his misgivings. Among the new acquaintances contracted by Beethoven since his arrival at Vienna was that of an excellent musician and thoroughly worthy man, Johann Schenk, himself a composer, who afterwards attained to some reputation as a writer of operas. As Beethoven was returning home one day from Haydn's house, the two met in the street, and fell into conversation. The young student was downcast at what he considered his small progress, and glad enough of any opportunity that might offer itself of confiding his grievances to a sympathetic ear. He carried in his portfolio the exercises that had just been submitted to his master, and Schenk looked over them there and then. To Beethoven's indignation and Schenk's astonishment, the pages were found to contain many a fault to which Haydn had omitted to draw his pupil's attention. Beethoven's first impulse was to throw up his lessons and cease all further connection with Haydn; but calmer and more politic counsels prevailed. An arrangement was finally concluded, in accordance with which Schenk was to supplement the tuition of Ludvig's ostensible master, correct the corrections, and generally help him along the thorny path of contrapuntal study. Beethoven's eager desire to become thoroughly grounded in the technicalities of his art shows that, masterful and "difficult" as he often was, he had no high-flown notions concerning the irresponsibility of pre-eminent talent, and realized to its full extent, even if he had never heard it, the significance of Buffon's dictum—*La génie n'est sòuvent qu'une longue patience.* The plan worked well, and a cordial friendship grew up between Beethoven and Schenk.

Subsequently, when Beethoven's hands and brain were full, they lost sight of one another. Although both continued to live in Vienna, each went his own way, and lived his own life; and the life that lay before Beethoven was one of too great self-absorption to leave much room for good-fellowship, or for the seeking out of old friends who for some reason or other failed to put in an appearance. Fickleness or forgetfulness of benefits received were not in his nature, however his actions may sometimes have been misconstrued. They did meet—once only, many years after—and by accident, as on that former occasion when Beethoven, on his way from Haydn's house, found the very mentor needed to help him out of his perplexities. At the sight of his old friend the heart of the now world-famous composer bounded with joy. Immediate adjournment to a neighbouring tavern was proposed and carried with alacrity. There, in a snug corner, forgetful of the busy world outside, the two passed several hours in half merry, half regretful converse, exchanging confidences, counting successes and failures, and reviving memories of those old days since which so many important events had occurred to change the complexion of both their lives. But more than ever those lives led in different directions. The old friends parted at the doors of the 'Jägerhorn,' never to meet again.

Absent-minded as he was, Beethoven forgot neither friends nor the kindnesses received from friends; and if at any time he had done them any real or fancied wrong, he continued to be tormented long afterwards by an exaggerated notion of the heinousness of his offence, and was unstinted in his expressions of contrition. This trait is illustrated in an affectionate, true-hearted, altogether charming letter written in 1793 to his old companion and almost sister, Eleanore von Breuning:—

"Often have I indulged in pleasant thoughts of you and your dear family; oftener still have I missed that peaceful feeling I should wish to experience whilst thus thinking of you. At such moments the memory of that fatal misunderstanding has risen before me, and my conduct in connection with it appeared to me more hateful than ever. But all that belongs to the past. What would I not give to be able to wipe out for ever the recollection of my conduct at that time!—so discreditable to me, and so opposed to the general tenor of my character! But many circumstances at that time contributed to our estrangement; and the main obstacles to our reconciliation, I suspect, were those persons who repeated to one remarks made by the other."

Nor does he forget to send a message to the pretty Barbara Koch.

"Tell her she is unkind not to have written to me even once. Twice have I written to her, and three times to Malchus—but no answer. Tell her that if she will not write to me herself, she might at least get Malchus to do so."

On another occasion, when sending Eleanore some variations, and a rondo with violin accompaniment, he again alludes to the old misunderstanding, the thought of which still weighed upon his mind—

"The pretty cravat worked by your hands caused me the greatest surprise. Pleased as I was, it aroused in me a feeling of melancholy. It reminded me of the past, and caused me to feel ashamed as I thought of your generous conduct. Indeed, I did not think you still considered me to be worthy of a place in your remembrance."

Several explanations have been attempted of the easy-going fashion in which Haydn, sometimes at any rate, directed the studies of his pupil. Beethoven, suspicious by nature, was often inclined to attribute this to intentional neglect, and never thoroughly forgave him. But Haydn was a busy man just then; possibly, too, as has been suggested, he may have been influenced by a vague feeling that in Beethoven he had an exceptional pupil, and one who, to a great extent, might be safely left to himself.

Thayer fixes the period during which Beethoven received supplementary lessons from Schenk between January 1793 and about the end of the year. In the summer of 1794 Haydn was in England, and Schenk staying at the seat of Count Auerspurg, busy with the composition and production of operas for the private theatre of his patron. According to Neefe, Haydn made Beethoven a definite proposal that he should accompany him on his English tour; but the latter, persisting in his notion that "he did not mean well towards him," did not take kindly to the plan. From a "diplomatic" letter—not dated, but believed to have been written in 1793—which Schenk found awaiting him at his lodgings, it will be seen that relations were not sufficiently strained to prevent Ludvig from accompanying his master on a visit to Eisenstadt, the country residence of Haydn's patron, Prince Esterhazy. Schenk was left in ignorance of this expedition until, calling at Beethoven's house, he found the following note—

"DEAR SCHENK,—I had no idea that I should be off to Eisenstadt to-day. I should have much liked to have one more chat with you. Meanwhile, count upon my gratitude for all the kindness you have shown to me. I will do all that lies in my power to requite it. I hope soon to see you again, and to enjoy the pleasure of your society. Farewell. Do not quite forget your
"BEETHOVEN."

Haydn's subsequent visit to England, and the absence of Schenk from Vienna on business of his own, removed any feeling of delicacy that may have prevented Beethoven hitherto from seeking further assistance in his studies. His choice fell upon Albrechtsberger. Under this learned, dry, but thorough teacher he submitted, for a period of about eighteen months, to a course of severe discipline in strict counterpoint, simple and double, free counterpoint, imitation, and all the intricacies of fugal composition. The painstaking manner in which Beethoven devoted himself to these tasks sufficiently shows that while, on occasions, he was not slow to manifest the independence of genius, the humility of genius was by no means wanting. His instructors may not have appreciated his declaration that "it was a good thing to learn occasionally what is according to rule, that hereafter one may come to what is contrary to rule"; but, at any rate, they must have seen clearly that in this speech there was no specious excuse for shirking the ordeal of study. Proofs of his industry at that time are still in existence, in the shape of some 263 exercises which were written on the above-named subjects, and which reflect equal credit upon the conscientiousness of master and pupil. Besides these theoretical studies, Beethoven sought the help of Salieri, director of the opera, and later on, court Capellmeister, in the art of writing for the voice. Ten of Beethoven's compositions, containing Salieri's corrections, have been published by Nottebohm. Till late in life Beethoven preserved the habit of referring many a question to his old adviser, and was never too proud to call himself "Salieri's pupil." He also took lessons—first on the viola, and then on the violin—from Schuppanzigh; from Kraft and Linke on the violoncello; from Friedlowsky on the clarionet; and Punto on the horn. It has to be confessed that Beethoven's mode of receiving instruction was of a kind likely to cause many of his teachers to eye him askance. As for Albrechtsberger the solid, whose susceptibilities must have suffered many a shock, he disposed of the matter summarily enough—"Don't have anything to do with him. He has learnt nothing, and will never do anything in decent style." In further confirmation of Beethoven's unpopularity with his masters—to which, however, there were several pleasant exceptions—Ries writes: "I know them all well. All three had a high regard for Beethoven, but only one opinion concerning his studies. They agreed that Beethoven was so obstinate and self-willed that he had to learn afterwards, through hard experience, many a truth he refused to accept from his teachers. This was especially the opinion of Albrechtsberger and Salieri." Haydn had dubbed Beethoven "the Great Mogul"; and this young student's now historic "*I* say it is right," in answer to Ries, when the latter cited distinguished authority against certain consecutive fifths in an early quartet, no doubt seemed to afford some justification of the nickname.

A few words now become necessary concerning some among the many persons in high places who speedily recognized Beethoven's worth and genius, opened their houses to him, placed him on the footing of personal friendship, tolerated his whims and even his occasional rudeness, and by their encouragement assisted—so far as such outside circumstances can be said to have influenced it—in making his career in Vienna what it was.

Among the first to come forward was the good-hearted, pompous Baron van Swieten, son of Maria Theresa's favourite physician—a very conspicuous figure indeed among the aristocratic amateurs of the day. Van Swieten had formerly been appointed ambassador to the Prussian Court. On his return to Vienna he succeeded his father as Prefect of the Public Library, and later became President of the Educational Commission. A musician of the old school, with tastes in the direction of the "grand and massive," he organized at his house, with the co-operation of Mozart, Sunday morning performances of classical music, including the choral works of Handel and Bach. He was also the founder of the *Musikalische Gesellschaft*, an association formed by twenty-five aristocratic amateurs for promoting a taste for music of the highest class. The Baron also turned his hand to composition, and produced, besides some songs, six symphonies, upon which Haydn's verdict was summed up in the words, "stiff as himself." His grand airs of patronage went down probably better with Haydn than with Haydn's pupil. It was by van Swieten's persuasion that the former was induced to introduce a realistic croaking of frogs in *The Seasons*—an ill turn that he never forgot or forgave. To Beethoven van Swieten proved a sincere and serviceable friend; and in spite of class distinctions, and his perpetual consciousness of them, relations of considerable intimacy appear to have gradually arisen between them. Musical meetings were held regularly at van Swieten's rooms, and often, after the guests had left, the young *protégé* was kept up, far into the small hours, to regale his host with half a dozen or so of Bach's fugues by way of *Abendsegen*—a fate of which he had fair warning in the wording of at least one of his invitations—"If nothing stands in the way, I should be glad to see you here next Wednesday at half-past eight o'clock, with your nightcap in your pocket."

In another influential house, where the early death of Mozart had left a blank not easy to fill, the young musician found two of his most faithful and generous supporters. These were the Prince Lichnowsky and his accomplished wife, formerly the beautiful Countess of Thun. Both had been the devoted friends of that great composer, the mantle of whose genius, according to Waldstein's prophecy, was destined to fall upon Beethoven's shoulders. Whether or not Beethoven may be said to have received this inheritance through the hands of Haydn, no doubt it was as Haydn's pupil that he first attracted the attention of the childless couple, and quickly succeeded to the place in their affection occupied by Mozart during his lifetime. Lichnowsky held quartet parties at his house every Friday; the regular performers being Schuppanzigh, Sina, Weiss, and Kraft, all of whom subsequently made their mark in the world. His entertainments were frequented by the chief notables in the world of music and fashion—in Viennese society of those days the two terms were synonymous—and even royalty was attracted to the house by the princess's charm of manner and intellectual conversation. An amateur pianist of some merit, she has been described by Schonfeld, a Viennese writer, as "a strong musician, who plays the pianoforte with feeling and expression." For Beethoven the princess became in time a second Madame von Breuning. Quickly recognizing his nobility of soul beneath the rugged exterior, she tolerated his foibles, his hatred of etiquette, his occasional outbursts of temper. She reproved his faults with mingled firmness and kindness; on occasions, also, played the part of mediator between her husband and his *protégé*, when, as was not infrequently the case, differences arose between them. In 1794 the Lichnowskys offered Beethoven a home in their palace, and for ten years he lived there as one of the family, his only complaint being that they took too much care of him. "They wanted," he playfully observed, "to train me there with *grandmotherly* love; and the princess would have liked to put me in a glass case that no evil might come nigh me."

Certainly the task of keeping within bounds a young genius so impatient of trammels, and so sensitively alive to any fancied interference with his independence, must have required no small tact and forbearance. Many hitches occurred at first, which were only to be surmounted by good-natured submission on the side of the patrons to the demands of their sometimes overbearing guest. Even the fixed dinner-hour of four o'clock was a grievance. Rather than be tied to this every day, Beethoven often forsook the princely table in favour of independence and the coarser fare of some neighbouring restaurant. When he wished to learn riding the prince's horses were placed at his disposal; but he would have none of them, and forthwith purchased a horse for himself. Little acts of courtesy, which were meant to appease rather than ruffle his sense of dignity, threw Beethoven into a fever of irritation. Whenever he and the prince happened to ring their bells at the same time, the latter would order the Jäger in his stentorian voice to attend first to the summons of his guest. Remarking this, Beethoven insisted upon engaging a servant for himself. Other misunderstandings, of a more serious kind, arose later, and threatened at one time to cause a permanent breach.

In musical matters Beethoven had a high opinion of Lichnowsky's judgment, and this went even to the length of submitting to his criticism. The prince was an efficient pianist, and took pleasure in tackling the executive difficulties presented by Beethoven's novel style of composition for that instrument, so that their artistic intercourse was mutually beneficial. For the rest, Lichnowsky may have been pardoned a feeling of legitimate pride in retaining, as a permanent guest in his house, the most remarkable pianist of the day.

Among various anecdotes illustrative of the princess's readiness to administer good-natured reproof when she thought it deserved, is one related by Ferdinand, son of the Beethovens' faithful old friend, Franz Ries. The incident occured some years later than the period we are now concerned with. Ferdinand, in miserable circumstances enough, had arrived in Vienna from Paris, bearing a letter of introduction from his father. He could have brought no better credentials. Beethoven consented to give him pianoforte lessons; but passed him over to Albrechtsberger for composition. He also helped him on occasions with money, and used influence to procure him sundry modest appointments that yielded sufficient at any rate to keep him from want. One evening, while playing before a large company, Ries had the misfortune to strike a wrong note, and his master visited the offence with a tap on the head with one finger. The young pupil's vexation—aroused by the publicity of the reproof rather than by its severity—did not escape the observant eye of the princess. It was now Beethoven's turn to play; and, as often happened, he began one of his own compositions rather carelessly. Standing immediately behind the player the princess, equal to the occasion, avenged this indignity inflicted by the strong upon the weak with a succession of smart blows, exclaiming at the same time—"If a pupil is to be punished with one finger for a single false note, the master, for worse faults, deserves the whole hand!" "Everybody laughed," says Ries, "and Beethoven first of all. He began again, and played admirably."

Installed in the Lichnowsky Palace, and left, in all essential matters, to his own devices, Beethoven must have found life not only tolerable, but on many occasions enjoyable. Free to come and go, and to dress as he liked, he passed the day in study, composition, and music teaching; the evenings either in the company of his patrons and their friends, or at one or other of the many aristocratic houses now open to him. A great source of artistic pleasure as well as improvement was his association with the celebrated Quartet—then called the Schuppanzigh, but known later as the Rasoumoffsky Quartet. In drilling the young performers, who were hereafter to be the interpreters of some of the grandest emanations of his genius in this department of music, Beethoven, in conjunction with Prince Lichnowsky, spared neither time nor trouble. For both it was a labour of love, and the result was an *ensemble* such, perhaps, as could have been obtained only under the guidance and inspiration of the composer himself.

The Archduke Rudolph may be said to be the single amateur among all his aristocratic acquaintance whom Beethoven consented to take seriously in hand as a pupil; and in making an exception in this case the composer, besides showing his discernment, laid the foundation of a lifelong friendship, productive of much pleasurable intercourse for both, and, on many an occasion, of incalculable value to himself. This amiable and accomplished nobleman—the grandchild of Maria Theresa, and nephew of the Elector, Max Franz—came of a musical stock, and himself possessed musical gifts of no mean order. He first commenced his studies under Beethoven in about 1804, when still a youth in his teens. The fact that in later life he was said to surmount successfully the difficulties of even the great B♭ Sonata, gives some idea of the proficiency he acquired as a pianist; while two published works show that he possessed talent also for composition. The pianoforte concertos in G and E♭, the great Sonata Op. 106, the pianoforte trio in B♭, and, above all, the colossal *Missa Solennis*, to be hereafter referred to, are among the important works dedicated to this friend and patron.

The biographical significance of the dedications affixed in so many instances to Beethoven's compositions will be appreciated when it is remembered that only by such means was it possible in those days for an artist to publicly express his gratitude for the friendship extended to him by influential patrons. A glance at these dedications is sufficient to recall many an important and stirring event in Beethoven's career, in connection not only with the aristocratic amateurs, the electors, princes, and courts, who rendered him more or less substantial services, but also with more romantic episodes.

Similarly, a fair idea can be obtained of the social surroundings acquired by Beethoven after he had lived a short time in Vienna, by passing in review some of the principal names attached to his works during the last decade of the eighteenth century, or shortly after. To mention a few of these, Prince Lobkowitz received the dedication of the first Quartets, Op. 18; Count Fries—another of his wealthy supporters with whom he was very intimate for a time—was associated with the Violin Sonatas, Op. 23 and 24, and the String Quintet, Op. 29. The Russian Count Browne (*le premier Mecene de sa Muse*, as Beethoven called him), and his wife; Prince Schwarzenberg; the Countess von Keglevics, and the Countess von Thun; Princess Esterhazy, and various others, also figure in the list.

The three pianoforte trios, Op. 1, dedicated to the prince, were performed for the first time at the Lichnowsky Palace in the presence of a brilliant gathering. The occasion was marked by one of those awkward incidents so frequently brought about by the total want of sympathy between Beethoven and his master. Amid the chorus of congratulations that followed the performance, Haydn stepped forward and warmly praised the two first trios, but recommended that the last (in C minor) should not be published. It was Beethoven's favourite of the three, and his feelings on hearing this advice are not difficult to imagine. Yet Haydn's verdict was no doubt sincere. The older composer had already reached the summit of his artistic aspirations, and was little disposed to believe in anything beyond. As for the sinister motives sometimes imputed to him by Beethoven, all that need be said is that there is no evidence of them. In a half-hearted way, Beethoven dedicated to the master his three pianoforte Sonatas, Op. 2, but he flatly refused to insert "Pupil of Haydn" on the title-page, declaring that "he had never learnt anything from him."

The high-born beauties of Vienna vied with each other in showering attentions upon their favourite, often to the detriment of his peace of mind. They paid visits to his lodgings, made him free of their houses, and tolerated bursts of ill-temper such as would have insured for ordinary men the ostracism of the polite world. Though his manners were never conventional, and sometimes outrageous, Beethoven's sterling character and commanding genius, together with a certain indescribable fascination peculiar to himself, atoned for all. His society friends did more than tolerate him; they esteemed and loved him.

Nevertheless, his roughness of bearing, his shabby dress ("quite a contrast to the elegant attire customary in our circles," says a young lady who met him at the Lichnowskys' in those days) must have caused him to present a strangely incongruous figure in the brilliant drawing-rooms he frequented; and when at his worst, his obstinacy and ill-humour, especially in later life, must have been hard to bear. "He was very proud," says the same eye-witness. "I have known him refuse to play even when the Countess Thun, the mother of Princess Lichnowsky, fell on her knees, as he lay on the sofa, to entreat him. The countess was a very eccentric woman."

Worse than this, however, is the account given by Ries of his proceedings on one occasion, when the two were playing a duet at the house of Count Browne. The performance was disturbed by a conversation between a nobleman and a young lady at the other end of the room. After several vain attempts had been made to still the disturbance, Beethoven became enraged, lifted his pupil's hands from the key-board, and said in a loud voice, "I play no longer for such hogs!" To storm at his young lady-pupils, tear their music into shreds, and scatter it about the room in the manner described by the Countess Gallenberg—all this, it will be pretty generally admitted, was carrying the prerogatives of genius to startling lengths.

With his brother professionals in Vienna—excepting, of course, those who were intimately associated with him—Beethoven was not on equally satisfactory terms. Many were annoyed by his masterful ways, or jealous of his social successes; many more were unable to understand his music. In the case of Beethoven the age of professional dandyism was of short duration, and his provincial dialect, his neglected attire and eccentric habits, made him the easy butt of a class of musicians who were not worthy to brush his shoes. In such company, however, Beethoven generally showed himself ready to give as good as he took.

In fact while music the art was, for Beethoven, the breath of life, music the profession, as generally understood, was actually distasteful to him. "I wish," he once said at Prince Lobkowitz's house, "I could rid myself of all necessity for bargaining with publishers, and meet with some one to pay me a settled income for life, on the understanding that the right of publishing everything I wrote should be his. I should not be idle. Terms of this sort, I believe, were made between Goethe and Cotta, and also between Handel and his London publishers." By this speech the "young musician from the Rhine" laid himself open to a cheap sarcasm, and one of his hearers promptly profited by the opportunity. "My dear young man," he replied, "what right have you to complain, seeing that you are neither a Goethe nor a Handel? It is not to be expected that masters like these will be born again." The host, Prince Lobkowitz, witnessed Beethoven's rage at this retort, and, later in the evening, tried to bring him to a calmer state of mind. "My dear Beethoven, the gentleman intended no offence. Every one admits that the present generation cannot reproduce the mighty spirits of the past." "I hold no intercourse with men who mistrust me because I am as yet unknown," was the reply: at which our informant says "there was much shaking of heads," and the young composer was generally voted presumptuous and overbearing.

Beethoven's personal appearance has been described

by his contemporaries with a minute particularity that makes it possible to arrive at a fairly clear conception of it. A rather short, strong figure; dark, abundant hair; face broad, and always shaven—not called handsome by his warmest admirers, but indicating power in every line, and capable of a remarkable play of expression; a face illumined by eyes that in moments of animation flashed from beneath the dome-like forehead; a face that could be gloomy, and at times forbidding, but that impressed those who learned to read it aright with a sense of childlike and lovable simplicity. His manner was often abrupt, and even aggressive. Perhaps he sometimes appeared so when nothing was further from his intention. A man with a C minor Symphony ringing in his head might well be excused some forgetfulness of the smaller conventionalities of life.

Hitherto Beethoven's playing in Vienna had been restricted to the drawing-rooms of his private friends. It was not till the year 1795 that the public, whose curiosity must have already been considerably excited by reports of the achievements of the young pianist from Bonn, had an opportunity of witnessing his powers. At the annual concert given at the Burg Theatre, for the benefit of the widows and orphans of musicians, the composer made his first public appearance. Salieri, as usual, conducted, and the programme included, besides an Operetta composed by one of his pupils, "a Pianoforte Concerto, in C major, by L. van Beethoven."

On this, as on several other occasions, Beethoven caused something like a panic among his friend's by postponing the completion of his composition till the last moment. Two days before the date of performance the Concerto was still in an unfinished state; one cause of the delay being an attack of colic, a malady to which the composer was subject. Wegeler was at hand to doctor him as well as he could; and while Beethoven, working at high pressure, filled sheet after sheet of music-paper, they were passed over to four copyists who attended in the next room. Next day at rehearsal a fresh *contretemps* arose. There was found to be a difference of half a tone between the pitch of pianoforte and that of the other instruments. To save a general retuning, Beethoven seated himself at the piano without hesitation, and played the whole Concerto in C sharp—not an entirely unprecedented feat, but nevertheless one that gives an idea of his thorough mastery over technical difficulties. Much of Beethoven's MS. was undecipherable to everybody but himself. Once during a public performance, when Seyfried was turning over for him, he noticed that the pages contained nothing but an inextricable jumble of notes, with an occasional bar filled in.

Other opportunities of playing before mixed audiences speedily presented themselves in entertainments organized for benevolent purposes—the chief *raison d'être* of public concerts held at Vienna in those days. At a performance for the benefit of Mozart's widow, held at the Burg Theatre a few days after his *début*, he played a concerto of the deceased master between the acts of *Clemenza di Tito*. Towards the end of the year, also, Beethoven co-operated in a public concert given by Haydn, and composed a series of minuets and waltzes to be played at a ball given by the "Society of Artists."

Although the flight of the Elector from Bonn, now in the hands of the French Revolutionary troops, had brought to an end once for all any designs Beethoven might have entertained of resuming his musical career in that place, a certain restlessness in his movements during 1796 would seem to indicate that he had not yet fully realized the fact that for the rest of his life Vienna was destined to be the scene of his labours and triumphs. That year was marked by an important event—a journey to Berlin, through Dresden and Leipzig. It was the only occasion on which he visited the northern capital, or indeed wandered any considerable distance from his head-quarters. In Berlin he obtained a gracious reception from Frederick William II.; played his two Sonatas for piano and violoncello before the court, and was presented by the king—himself a violoncellist—with a snuff-box full of Friedrichs d'or. "Not an ordinary snuff-box," he would explain when showing it to his friends, as he was rather fond of doing; "but one like those usually presented to ambassadors."

Great as was the enthusiasm excited in various circles by Beethoven's appearance in Berlin, and successful, on the whole, as was his visit there, it nevertheless brought with it some disappointments. One such arose from what he observed of the tone of music prevailing in circles he had been wont to look upon as the stronghold of classicism, but in which, with much talk about Bach and Handel, the Italian style reigned supreme. He greatly esteemed, however, the chivalric, art-loving Prince Louis Ferdinand, of whose playing he remarked: "It was not kingly nor princely, but only that of a good pianist."

In Berlin, as elsewhere, it was by his brilliant improvisation that Beethoven ousted all competitors—that improvisation of which Czerny said: "No matter in what society he was thrown, he made such an impression on all his hearers that frequently not a dry eye was to be seen, and many broke into sobs. There was something wonderful in his expression, besides the beauty and originality of his ideas." But according to the unanimous testimony of contemporaries, the effect of Beethoven's playing—whether extempore or in set compositions—depended less upon its technical merits than upon its inspirational character. When seated at the piano he seemed gradually to lose consciousness of all around him, and in the sounds he drew from it every shade of musical emotion obtained expression. Whether he was heard at his best or at his worst, the subtle charm of what a late eminent critic used to be fond of calling "the composer's touch," was never absent from his performance.

At the Berlin Academy, where he played twice with immense success, Beethoven was brought into contact with the conductor Fasch, and also with his successor Zelter, the friend of Goethe. The impression made upon him by the two leading representatives of high-class music in Berlin, confirmed his suspicion that here was not a place in which his genius could thrive or find worthy development; and he was quite content to leave the reigning favourites, Himmel and Righini, in undisturbed possession of the field. Before leaving the capital, however, he had the misfortune to give mortal offence to one of the pair. Himmel was also an extempore performer, and nothing loth to comply with Beethoven's request that he would give a specimen of his powers. Runs, progressions, arpeggios, endless preludizing—all the phenomena in fact of conventional improvisation—were turned off with the usual facility; but when he had nearly come to the end of his inspiration, Beethoven grew impatient, and brought matters to a crisis by exclaiming—"Do begin now." The sting of these words, which may well have fallen from his lips without any malicious intent, rankled ever afterwards in the soul of Himmel.

With plans for the future more clearly defined than they had been before his departure, Beethoven returned to Vienna; and, except to fulfil concert engagements or to recruit his health in the country, never again left it. The capital was full of excitement and alarm caused by the victories of Napoleon in Northern and Southern Italy; and Beethoven wrote a patriotic song of *Farewell* to the volunteers before their departure. His old Bonn companions, Bernhard Romberg and his cousin Andreas, driven home by the disturbed state of Italy, passed through Vienna at the end of the year, and gave a concert at which Beethoven played for them.

In return for twelve variations on a Russian dance, Count Browne presented the composer with a horse, which he rode for a few times and then completely forgot, until a reminder of its existence in the shape of a formidable bill for provender was presented. Meanwhile his servant had turned the master's absence of mind to profitable account by hiring out the animal for his own benefit.

Thayer gives reasons for fixing the year of 1797 as the date of a serious illness which overtook Beethoven, notwithstanding that Baron van Zmeskall's account of it, or rather of its supposed cause, relegates it to the year before. Zmeskall relates how Beethoven came home one summer day almost overpowered by the heat, threw open the doors and windows, took off his coat and vest, and sat at the window to cool himself; and how, as a consequence of this imprudence, he contracted a dangerous illness which "eventually settled on the organs of hearing"; but the full particulars of this occurrence have not been recorded.

Among the publications of this year figures the world-famous setting of Matthison's words *Adelaide*. It was not until the summer of 1800 that Beethoven sent a copy to the poet, accompanied by the following letter—

"MOST ESTEEMED FRIEND,

"With this you will receive a composition of mine which was printed several years ago, though to my shame you may possibly be unaware of its existence.

"In order to exculpate myself, and at the same time to explain how it happened that I dedicated something to you which came so entirely from my heart, without informing you of it, I may perhaps say, first, that I did not know where you were living, and then that I began to think, in my modesty, that I had acted over hastily in dedicating anything to you without first submitting it to your approval. Even now, indeed, it is with some diffidence that I send you *Adelaide*. *You* will well know what changes are brought about in an artist who is ever advancing; the more one achieves in art the less contented is he with former works.

"My most ardent desires will be fulfilled should you not be wholly dissatisfied with the music wedded to your heavenly *Adelaide:* and if this should impel you soon to write another poem of the same kind, and (if my request be not too bold) to send it to me at once, I will exert my best powers to approach the merit of your exquisite verse.

"Regard this dedication as a tribute of esteem and thankfulness for the intense pleasure I have found and always shall find in your poetry.

"When playing *Adelaide* think sometimes of

"Your sincere admirer,

"BEETHOVEN."

As was to be expected, Beethoven did not step into the foremost place among the *virtuosi* of Vienna without opposition; but at this distance of time, the attempts that were made to pit against him in serious rivalry two musicians of the calibre of Woelff and Steibelt seem almost incredible. The competition would have been more intelligible had the question at issue been one of mere executive skill; for Woelff, with his long fingers and dashing style, possessed powers of bravura well calculated to dazzle amateurs of a certain class. As in the somewhat parallel cases—always inevitably referred to—of Gluck and Piccini in Paris, and of Handel and

Buononcini in London, the little war was carried on by adherents on either side with a bitterness altogether incommensurate with its importance.

A contest, if it may be so called, took place at the villa of Woelff's patron, Count Wetzlar, when their pianos were placed side by side; the mere *virtuoso* surpassing himself in the display of his immense technique; while the composer speedily brought the audience under the spell of his poetical imagination. Woelff, however, in the opinion of his supporters, could still fairly claim superiority as an executant. On the whole this trial of skill between them appears to have been conducted in a friendly spirit, and although Woelff came off second best as far as the higher qualities of musicianship were concerned, he accepted the position with a grace that compares favourably with the jealous rage and overweening conceit exhibited by Steibelt under somewhat similar circumstances. The two met on other occasions at Count Wetzlar's house, and extemporized together. In commemoration of these times Woelff dedicated to Beethoven one of his sonatas; but the compliment was never returned.

The competition between Beethoven and Steibelt some years later (in 1800) occurred under less formal conditions, but was equally decisive in result—much to the astonishment of the new rival, fresh from his triumphs in Paris and Prague, who looked forward to an easy victory, and did not even take the trouble to call upon Beethoven after his arrival at the capital. They met by accident at the house of Count Fries, when

Beethoven played for the first time his Trio in B flat major, Op. 11, for piano, clarinet, and violoncello. The work does not offer much opportunity for display, "and Steibelt," says Ferdinand Ries, "listened condescendingly, and sure of gaining the day, paid several compliments to Beethoven. After playing in a quintet of his own composition he proceeded to improvise, and caused some sensation with his free shake—a novelty in those days. To ask Beethoven to play once more was out of the question."

A week afterwards a second concert was given at the house of Count Fries, when Steibelt repeated his success in another quintet. He had, also, carefully prepared a showy impromptu, upon a theme in the last movement of Beethoven's trio, much to the disgust of both the composer and his admirers. The turn of Beethoven came next; and he seated himself at the instrument in his accustomed manner—"rather pettishly, if one might say so, as if some one had pushed him there." On his way he snatched up the violoncello part of Steibelt's quintet; placed it at the piano upside down ("purposely?" asks Ries), and drummed away at the theme of the opening bars with one finger.

"Growing excited, Beethoven extemporized with such power that, before he had finished, Steibelt left the room. Since that incident whenever Steibelt was asked anywhere, one of his stipulations before accepting was that Beethoven should not be present."

There was evidently a good deal of human nature in Steibelt—especially of the kind so often attributed to the musical fraternity. Disgusted with the comparative coldness of his reception in Vienna, he returned to Paris in August of the same year.

In 1800 Beethoven commenced the habit, henceforth systematioally adhered to, of transferring his quarters during the autumn from Vienna to the country. He chose lodgings in the village of Unter-Döbling, a few miles from the capital, where, in the same house, lived an advocate named Grillparzer (father of the dramatic poet), and his wife and children. Even there the solitude so dear to composers—and to Beethoven more than others—was not always to be depended upon. Frau Grillparzer, a woman of cultivated musical taste, was caught outside the room listening to confidences meant for his piano alone. It was not the first time she and her son had stepped stealthily up-stairs with this nefarious intent; but it was the last. In vain was a message sent, through the servant, that she and her family would make a point of going for a walk whenever the master began to play. From that date no more music issued from the room. In fact listeners, on either side of the door, were Beethoven's pet aversion, and he often asserted the fact in characteristically unceremonious fashion. Even his young pupil Ries was debarred presently from the privilege of hearing him play at home in consequence of a joke perpetrated upon the master by Lichnowsky.

Beethoven happened to play the theme of the Andante in E when Ries and Krumpholz were in his room. It made a vivid impression upon both, and shortly afterwards Ries, when on a visit to Lichnowsky, could not resist the temptation of playing it to him from memory.

Lichnowsky, equally taken with the music, also worked it out upon the piano for himself, and the next day when he saw Beethoven, waggishly asked him to listen to "something he had just composed." Far from entering into the spirit of the joke, Beethoven flew into a violent passion, and from that time, or shortly after, refused to play before his patron's friends.

Beethoven's periodical escapes from the bustle of town to the green fields and fresh air of the country, must have been the chosen times for his purest and noblest inspirations. How he revelled in the beauties of nature, and to what imaginative uses he applied them is amply shown, not only in the well-known *Pastoral Symphony*, and in the *Pastoral Sonata*—aptly so called by the publishers, though Beethoven himself did not furnish that title—but in many another work of priceless beauty. During his stay at Unter-Döbling, one among other matters that occupied his attention was the shaping and development of his ideas for the *Prometheus Ballet*—produced with immense success at the Burg Theatre in March of the following year. On the day following its performance we read of yet another of those little skirmishes between Beethoven and Haydn, in which they seemed to indulge with a sort of zest on every convenient opportunity. The two happen to meet in the street; and this time, as the dialogue is recorded, Beethoven appears to fire the first shot; for Haydn commences, innocently enough, with congratulations and an assurance that the *Prometheus Ballet* pleased him very much. Beethoven's reply is enigmatical and slightly irritating—" O *lieber Päpa,* you are too good! But its no 'creation.'" To which Papa Haydn retorts—"No. It is no 'creation,' and I don't think it ever will be." And with this exchange of amenities they part. The title of the ballet in question, it will be remembered, was *Die Geschöpfe des Prometheus.*

In 1800 Beethoven had already quitted the hospitable shelter of the Lichnowsky Palace for lodgings in a house *im tiefen Graben*, where, with less luxury but greater freedom, he could follow his career under conditions evidently felt by him to be more suitable. Here Charles Czerny, the future teacher of Liszt, but then about ten years old, was taken to see Beethoven in pursuance of a long-standing promise; and in an account of the interview written by him years after, he has given a picture of Beethoven as he appears at that time in his work-a-day garb.

"I was about ten years old when Krumpholz took me to see Beethoven. What a day of mingled joy and trepidation for me was that on which I was to see the renowned master! Even now the excitement of that moment comes back to me. On a winter day we sallied forth—my father, Krumpholz, and I—from the Leopoldstadt, where we were still living, to the street called 'Tiefen Graben,' and mounted to the fifth or sixth story, where a somewhat slatternly servant announced us, and then disappeared. We entered a veritable desert of a room—papers and clothes scattered about—some trunks—bare walls, scarcely a chair except the rickety one before the Walter piano (at that time considered the best). Six or eight persons were in the room. Among them the two brothers Wranitzky,

Süssmayer, Schuppanzigh, and one of Beethoven's brothers.

"Beethoven was dressed in a dark gray jacket and trousers of some long-haired material, which reminded me of the description of Robinson Crusoe I had just been reading. The jet black hair (*à la Titus*) stood upright on his head. A beard, unshaven for several days, made still darker his naturally swarthy face. I noticed also, with a child's quick perception, that he had cotton wool which seemed to have been dipped in some yellow fluid in both ears. . . . His hands were covered with hair, and the fingers very broad, especially at the tips." For a time Czerny became Beethoven's pupil, and he has given some interesting recollections of the master's mode of teaching:—"Beethoven," he says, "devoted the first few lessons to scales in all the keys, and showed me (what at that time most players were ignorant of) the only good position of the hands and fingers, and especially the use of the thumb—rules whose full purport I only understood in after years. Then he took me through the exercises in Bach's book, making me pay particular attention to the *legato*, of which he was so unrivalled a master, but which at that time—the Mozart period, when the short *staccato* touch was in fashion—all other pianists thought impossible. Beethoven told me afterwards that he had often heard Mozart, whose style, from his use of the clavecin—the piano being in his time in its infancy—was not at all adapted to the newer instrument."

In 1801 Beethoven moved from the *tiefen-Graben* to higher ground in the *Sailer-stätte*, whence his lodgings commanded a good view over the ramparts; and that and several other summers were spent at the picturesque village of Hetzendorf, near the Imperial summer palace of Schönbrunn, where his first patron, the Elector, had found quiet retreat after the turmoil and fever of the latter part of his reign at Bonn. There, also, wandering among the avenues and glades of the park, note-book ever in hand, the composer forgot his deafness, his worries, his ill-fated loves, in that other world of sound to which his true life belonged. Years afterwards he revisited with Schindler the scene hallowed to his memory by many an association, and pointed out his favourite seat between two leafy boughs of an old oak tree. The *Mount of Olives* (not produced till 1803) was in progress at about this time. This first and only oratorio achieved a notable success, in spite of Huber's somewhat theatrical treatment of the purely religious ideas to which the work was devoted.

Among the dedications with a "history" attached to them is that of the Sonata in C♯ minor—popularly known as the *Moonlight* Sonata. Concerning the beautiful Countess Giulietta Guicciardi, and the romance which novelists and biographers have delighted to weave around Beethoven's intercourse with her, the ever minute and painstaking Thayer has much to say. After making due allowance for exaggeration, and for some inaccuracies of detail in the currently accepted account of the dedication, this must still be regarded as one of the most serious of Beethoven's many romantic attachments. The wife of the Imperial Counsellor, Count Guicciardi, was connected with the Hungarian family of the Brunswicks—always staunch friends of the composer. When their daughter Giulietta first took music lessons of Beethoven, she was in her seventeenth year

—rather a dangerous state of things, it will be admitted, considering the susceptibility of the master and the attractive qualities of his enthusiastic pupil. Matters were further complicated by the fact that Giulietta was already as good as affianced to Count Gallenberg, an impresario, and composer of ballet music, although the financial position of this nobleman was so unsatisfactory, that for some time Giulietta's father refused consent to the match. At least on one occasion we hear of Beethoven coming forward to help his rival out of a money difficulty. For a season, at any rate, Beethoven's star was in the ascendant in the affections of this charming girl; and, despite the disparity of their social position, the possibility of marriage must at one time have crossed his mind. Such hopes, however, were quickly disturbed, as will be seen from a passage in a letter written to Wegeler this year, in which reference is evidently made to Giulietta.

In the opinion of many persons, some light has been thrown upon this love episode by the contents of two sheets of note-paper which were found in a secret drawer, together with some bank shares, after Beethoven's death. They bore no name, nor any indication of the year in which they were written, but only the dates, "July 6, morning," and "Monday, July 6, evening," and they began as follows—

"My Angel, my All, Myself,—A few words only to-day in pencil—thy pencil. My lodging will not be definitely fixed before to-morrow. What miserable waste of time! Why this deep grief when necessity speaks? Can our love exist except by sacrifice, by not demanding all; can you help not being quite mine, I not quite thine? Ah, God! Look into beautiful nature, and calm thy mind over what must be. Love demands all, and justly; so it is from me to thee and from thee to me; only thou forgettest that I must live for myself and for thee. Were we quite united thou wouldest feel this grief no more than I. . . . My journey was terrible. I did not arrive till four in the morning; for want of sufficient horses the mail-coach chose a different route, and what a terrible road! At the last station they warned me not to travel at night, and frightened me with a wood; but that only tempted me, and I was wrong. The carriage could not but collapse in the terrible road, bottomless, a mere country road; but for my postilions I should have stuck there.

"Esterhazy with eight horses on the usual route had the same fate that I had with four; and yet I felt a certain sensation of pleasure, as I always do when successfully battling with a difficulty—now quickly, from the external to the internal. We shall probably see one another soon, and to-day I cannot tell you the thoughts I had regarding my life during these few days. Were our hearts but always close together I should have none such. My heart is full; I have much to say to thee. Oh! there are moments when I find that language is nothing. Be cheerful; remain my faithful sole treasure, my all, as I am thine; the rest the gods must send, what shall be and must be.

"Thy faithful

"LUDVIG."

The rest is equally full of endearing epithets, vehement protestations, and passionate appeals; repeated again on the sheet dated 7th July, which has a postscript—

"Ever mine!
"Ever thine!
"Ever each other's!"

Whoever may have been the intended recipient of this impassioned, at times incoherent, effusion (in which are used throughout the more intimate "Du" and "Deinem"), it was manifestly penned under the influence of unwonted emotion. Schindler does not hesitate to connect it with the beautiful Giulietta; Thayer, on the other hand, makes havoc with some but not all the reasons that might seem to favour this conjecture. He shows, for example, that, of all the years that need be taken into the calculation, 1807 is the only one containing a "Monday, 6 July"; and after giving other arguments why this cannot have been the year, he goes on to assume that Beethoven, in his letter, made a mistake of one day, and settles upon 1806 (when Giulietta, then Countess of Gallenberg, was away at Naples) as the real date; thus strengthening the case for his own pretender, the Countess Theresa of Brunswick. But, as a more recent commentator has pointed out, once admit this latitude and the whole chronological argument falls to the ground. There is really no conclusive reason why the letter should not have been written in 1802, before Giulietta had become Countess of Gallenberg and left Naples. With regard to the C♯ minor Sonata, however, all the pretty legends attached to it are destroyed, as far as Giulietta is concerned, by her own account of the dedication, and this has been ruthlessly applied to his argument by Thayer. "Beethoven gave me the Rondo in G," she said years afterwards to Otto Jahn, "but wishing to dedicate something to Princess Lichnowsky, he gave me the Sonata instead." Whether or not the "immortal loved one" and Giulietta Guicciardi were one and the same person, there is ample evidence of the reality and intensity of Beethoven's passion; and little cause for surprise at his revulsion of feeling when she subsequently married Count Gallenberg.

Once, many years afterwards when all this sorrow belonged to past history, Beethoven when talking to his friend Schindler revived the subject of the long-lost Giulietta. Their conversation occurred in a public place, and was carried on in writing; for Beethoven, like many other deaf persons, "did not like to trust his own voice."

His communications, by way of further precaution, were couched in the curious and not very lucid French peculiar to him:—"J'étais bien aimé d'elle," he writes, "et plus que jamais, son époux. Il était plus son amant que moi, mais par elle j'apprenais de son misère, et je trouvais un homme de bien, qui me donnait la somme de 500 florins pour le soulager. Il était toujours mon enemi c'était justement la raison que je fusse (*sic*) tout le bien que possible. . . . Elle était née Guicciardi. Elle était l'épouse de lui avant son voyage en Italie—arrivé à Vienne elle cherchait moi pleurant, mais je la méprisois."

Already in 1801 apprehensions of that terrible malady

which cast a gloom over the latter part of Beethoven's career, and turned it into a veritable life-tragedy, began to take ominous shape. The dreaded symptoms grew ever more unmistakable. Beethoven, to whom the faculty of hearing was more precious than, perhaps, to any other man in the world, was gradually becoming deaf. The dark thoughts which beset him when first he realized the full extent of this calamity, and the fortitude with which he struggled against them; his noble resolve that even when dead to the world he would live for his art,—all this is touchingly set forth in two deeply interesting letters addressed to his friend Wegeler.

Wegeler has placed the first of these letters in 1800; the fact has been clearly established that both were written in the year 1801. The first, dated 29th June, abounds in assurances of unabated friendship, and affectionate references to the companions he had left behind. "It will be for me one of the happiest days of my life when I am once more able to see you, and to greet our Father Rhine." Of his worldly prospects at that time he writes in a cheerful strain. "They are, after all, not so bad. Lichnowsky still remains my warmest friend, difficult as it may be for you to believe it. As for those little squabbles, did they not serve rather to bring us closer together? Since last year he has secured me a pension of six hundred guldens, which I am to draw until I can obtain a suitable appointment. I make much money by my compositions; indeed, I may say that more demands are made upon me than I am able to attend to; and that for each of my works there are six or seven publishers; and if I liked I could have more. They no longer bargain with me; I demand, and they pay. This you see is a capital thing. For instance, if I see a friend in distress, and have no money at hand to help him, all I have to do is to sit down and write, and he is soon relieved." But when he approaches the subject of health his tone changes to one of deep despondency. Various doctors, among them the army-surgeon Vering, have ordered strengthening medicine, oil of almonds, tepid Danube baths,—but all have been tried in vain, or with but temporary success. "My life, I may say, passes miserably; for nearly two years I have shunned society, because I cannot bring myself to say to people, '*I am deaf.*' In other professions this would not be so much matter; for a musician it is terrible. Besides, what would my enemies say of this?—and I have not a few! That you may better realize the nature of this extraordinary deafness, I must tell you that when in the theatre I have to lean forward close to the orchestra before I can understand what the actors are saying. A little way off I cannot distinguish the high tones of musical instruments and voices. Strangely enough, in conversation people do not observe it; they attribute all to my frequent fits of absence. Often I can hear the tones but not the words of some one who speaks in a low voice; yet as soon as he begins to shout it is unbearable. How it will all end God alone knows. . . I am resolved, if it be possible, to defy my fate; although a time may come when I shall be the most wretched of God's creatures!" In the same letter he begs Wegeler to send him the portrait of his grandfather, the good old Capellmeister.

In the second, written three months later, Beethoven, after again describing his deafness and the treatment recommended by various doctors, touches upon another matter.

"Just now my life is somewhat pleasanter, and I mix more with other people. . . . This transformation has been wrought by a beautiful, fascinating girl who loves me, and is loved by me. Again, now that two years have passed away, have I experienced some joyful moments, and I begin for the first time to realize the happiness that marriage can bestow. But, alas! she moves in a circle far above me. At present, therefore, marriage for me is out of the question."

The "fascinating girl" here alluded to was, undoubtedly, Giulietta Guicciardi.

Carl and Johann Beethoven, naturally attracted by the success of their brother, soon followed him to Vienna. Schindler has described these two as the "evil principles" of the composer's life, and certainly the powerful ascendancy they managed to obtain over him had already wrought much trouble, and was fated in the future to cause more. From a purely mercantile view the help they afforded in negotiating with publishers was, no doubt, often valuable; but even in this respect their anxiety to convert everything into cash led to many transactions the reverse of beneficial to Beethoven's own interest as an artist. The composer's one serious quarrel with his brothers, of which any record exists, arose from their causing early pieces to be published which it was his intention to keep back as unworthy of his name. But what was even worse, they stood between Beethoven and his friends, meddled in his quarrels, fanned his anger when they ought to have allayed it, and often goaded him into doing and saying things he afterwards bitterly repented. Frequent attempts were made by the more sagacious of Beethoven's friends to withdraw him from this sinister influence, but always without success. "After all," he would say, "they are my brothers."

A certain sly amusement at their vanity and officiousness mingled with this forbearance, and he enjoyed giving them an occasional home-thrust. Later in life, when Brother Johann, the apothecary, a niggardly man by nature, had blossomed into a "country gentleman," as far as money could make him one, he sent Beethoven a card by way of New Year's greeting, on which he was unable to resist the temptation of inscribing himself—

"JOHANN VAN BEETHOVEN—*Land Proprietor*."

Schindler says of the composer's laugh that it was "too loud, and distorted his strongly-marked features." It is not difficult to imagine the uproarious mirth with which he turned over this missive, and after writing on the other side—

"LUDVIG VAN BEETHOVEN—*Brain Proprietor*"—

returned it to his brother Johann.

As the deafness grew worse, Beethoven consulted many doctors, passing successively under the care of his friend Wegeler, Vering, and others, and from them to Schmidt, professor of medicine at the Académie Joséphine. In 1802 he again changed his summer residence, this time for the secluded village of Heiligenstadt, farther away than Unter-Döbling, and in the same direction. He remained there till October, abandoning himself to the calm influences of nature, to his music, and also, unfortunately, to his own melancholy thoughts; but busy at the same time with composition, and not altogether unhappy in that other world of imagination in which his harassed spirit never sought refuge and consolation in vain. There, also, and in that year, Beethoven wrote the ineffably touching letter generally known as his "Will." It was addressed—

"TO MY BROTHERS CARL AND ——.

"*To be read and acted upon after my death.*

"To my brothers CARL and —— BEETHOVEN.

"O ye who think or say that I am rancorous, obstinate, or misanthropical, what an injustice you do me! You little know the hidden cause of my appearing so. From childhood my heart and mind have been devoted to benevolent feelings, and to thoughts of great deeds to be achieved in the future. But only remember that for six years I have been the victim of a terrible calamity, aggravated by incompetent doctors; led on from year to year by hopes of cure, and at last brought face to face with the prospect of a lingering malady, the cure of which may last for years, or may be altogether impossible. Born with an ardent, lively temperament fond of social pleasures, I was early compelled to withdraw myself, and live a life of isolation from all men

At times when I made an effort to overcome the difficulty, oh how cruelly was I frustrated by the doubly painful experience of my defective hearing! And yet it was impossible for me to say to people, 'Speak louder; shout, for I am deaf.' Ah, how was it possible I could acknowledge weakness in the very sense which ought to be more acute in my case than in that of others!—a sense which at one time I possessed in a perfection to which few others in my profession have attained, or are likely to attain. Oh, this I can never do! Forgive me, then, if you see me turn away when I would gladly mix with you. Doubly painful is my misfortune, seeing that it is the cause of my being misunderstood. For me there can be no recreation in human intercourse, no conversation, no exchange of thoughts with my fellow-men. In solitary exile I am compelled to live. Whenever I approach strangers I am overcome by a feverish dread of betraying my condition. Thus has it been with me throughout the past six months I have just passed in the country. The injunction of my intelligent physician, that I should spare my sense of hearing as much as possible, well accorded with my actual state of mind; although my longing for society has often tempted me into it. But how humbled have I felt when some one near me has heard the distant sounds of a flute, and I have heard *nothing;* when some one has heard a shepherd singing, and again I have heard *nothing!* Such occurrences brought me to the border of despair, and I came very near to putting an end to my own life. Art alone restrained me! Ah! it seemed impossible for me to quit this world for ever before I had done all I felt I was destined to accomplish. And so I clave to this distressful life; a life so truly miserable that any sudden change is capable of throwing me out of the happiest condition of mind into the worst. Patience! I must now choose her for my guide! This I have done. I hope to remain firm in my resolve, until it shall please the relentless Fates to cut the thread of life. Perhaps I shall get better; perhaps not. I am prepared. To have to turn philosopher in my twenty-eighth year! It is no easy task—harder for the artist than for any one else. O God, Thou lookest down upon my inward soul; Thou knowest, Thou seest that love for my fellow-men, and all kindly feelings have their abode there!

"O ye who may one day read this, remember that you did me an injustice; and let the unhappy take heart when he finds one like himself who, in spite of all natural impediments, has done all that was in his power to secure for himself a place in the ranks of worthy artists and men. My brothers, Carl and ——, as soon as I am dead request Dr. Schmidt in my name, if he be still alive, to describe my disease, and to add to these pages the history of my ailments, in order that the world, so far at least as is possible, may be reconciled to me after my death.

"Hereby I declare you both to be heirs of my little fortune (if it may so be called). Divide it honestly; bear with and help one another. The injuries you have done me I have, as you know, long since forgiven. You, brother Carl, I thank specially for the attachment you have shown towards me in these latter days. My wish is that your life may be more free from care than mine has been. Recommend Virtue to your children. She alone, not money, can give happiness. I speak from experience. It was she alone who raised me in the time of trouble; and I thank her, as well as my art, that I did not seek to end my life by suicide. Farewell, and love one another. I thank all friends, especially Prince Lichnowsky and Professor Schmidt.

The instruments from Prince L—— I should like to be kept by one of you; but let there be no quarrelling between you in regard to this. As soon as you can turn them to more useful purpose, sell them. How happy shall I be if even when in my grave I can be useful to you!

"And thus it has happened. Joyfully I hasten to meet death. Should he come before I have had the opportunity of developing the whole of my artistic capacity, he will have come too soon in spite of my hard fate, and I shall wish he had come a little later. But even in that case I shall be content. Will he not release me from a state of endless misery? Come when thou will'st! I go to meet thee with a brave heart. Farewell, and do not quite forget me even in death! I have deserved this, since during my lifetime I have often thought of you, and tried to make you happy. So be it.

"LUDVIG VAN BEETHOVEN.

"*Heiligenstadt, 6th October*, 1802."

"*Heiligenstadt*, 10*th October*, 1802.—So I take leave of thee, sorrowfully enough. Even the cherished hope, which I brought here with me of being cured, at least to a certain extent, has now utterly forsaken me. It has faded like the fallen leaves of autumn. Almost as I came here so do I depart. Even the lofty hope that upheld me during the beautiful summer days has vanished. O Providence! let one more day of pure joy be vouchsafed to me! The echo of true happiness has so long been a stranger to my heart!—When, when, O God! shall I again be able to feel it in the temple of nature and of man? Never?—no!—O that were too hard!"[1]

[1] It will be remarked that the name of his brother Johann does not appear in this document. The omission has been explained in more than one way, but has probably some connection with the unpleasantness referred to.

One is glad to believe that many of the painful passages in this "Promemoria" were written in a moment of unusual depression, and do not fairly represent Beethoven's general condition of mind at the time. Some warrant for this supposition seems afforded by the activity with which composition was still carried on, by the absence of anything like a sorrowful tone in much of the music belonging to the same year, and by other indications—such as the humorous letters to his quaint friend, the Baron Zmeskall, between whom and himself an interchange of harmless chaff was habitually carried on. One specimen of this correspondence may be given. Though short, and belonging to a later date, it fairly represents the rest. From their style we may infer that the man addressed was an oddity—and a good-natured one—at whom Beethoven, when in good spirits, felt free to poke his fun without fear of offence.

"MOST HIGH-BORN OF MEN!

"We beg of you to favour us with some goose-quills; and in return we will send you a whole bunch of the same kind, that you may not be obliged to pluck out your own. It is just possible that you may receive the Grand Cross of the Order of the Violoncello.

"We remain, your gracious and most gracious of all friends,

"BEETHOVEN."

Back in Vienna among his old friends, from whom it seems a pity he should have been so long isolated, Beethoven was soon, among other things, busy with the correction of publishers' proofs—no light labour in those days, when, to use his own expression, "errors swarmed in them like fish in the sea." But besides mistakes pure and simple, Beethoven had to deal also with still more irritating "improvements" of publishers. One offender of this sort, Nägeli of Zurich, incurred the composer's just resentment by supplying four bars of his own to the Sonata in G, Op. 31; and other works at different times suffered similar outrage.

In the same autumn Beethoven again changed his lodging, choosing this time an upper story in the Petersplatz, one of the busiest quarters of Vienna. He may have been influenced in this choice by the fact that his old friend and instructor in quartet-writing, Aloys Förster, occupied the floor above him. Förster's son, then a boy six years old, retained in after life a vivid and not altogether agreeable recollection of dreary winter mornings, when he had to descend to the master's room at six o'clock, shivering with cold, for a pianoforte lesson.

Lovers of music living in Vienna in April 1803 enjoyed the privilege of attending what may be called indeed an important concert. The programme contained no less than three new works—the *Mount of Olives* already referred to, the Symphony in D, and the Pianoforte Concerto in C minor, with Beethoven himself for pianist! The last rehearsal took place in the theatre at eight o'clock in the morning—"A terrible rehearsal," says Ries, "and by half-past two everybody was tired out and more or less discontented." But the genial Lichnowsky, who was present from the beginning, had brought some huge baskets laden with meat, wine, and bread-and-butter, and he was soon hard at work, pressing the good things upon each tired musician with both his friendly hands. After this all went well."

Among other important compositions introduced to the Viennese public this year was the well-known Kreutzer Sonata, originally written for a violinist with the English-sounding name of Bridgetower, the son of a negro and a Polish lady. His father lived in London, and was known there as the "Abyssinian Prince." In Vienna the young violinist generally passed as an Englishman—in itself, no doubt, a recommendation in Beethoven's eyes. According to his own testimony, Bridgetower had rendered the work to the composer's entire satisfaction, but from another witness we have a different account. "Bridgetower," he says, "was a mulatto, and played in a very extravagant style. When he performed the Sonata with Beethoven it was received with fits of laughter." However this may be, a quarrel arose between the two—according to the violinist "about a girl"—and the dedication was transferred to R. Kreutzer, a violinist who had been attached to the establishment of Bernadotte the French ambassador.

Active work, and numerous social engagements during this winter, may be supposed to have had the salutary effect of diverting Beethoven's mind from gloomy forebodings. Besides making acquaintance with Breuning's friend Gleichenstein, and with Mähler, and the artist Macco, he associated a good deal with the Abbé Vogler (then on a visit to Vienna with his pupil, Carl von Weber), the two exchanging subjects for improvisation, or playing together in friendly rivalry.

In the early part of 1803 Beethoven entered into negotiations with Schikaneder, then manager of the Theatre *An der Wien*, with regard to a new opera; but although the agreement was so far completed that he quitted his lodgings in the Petersplatz, and installed himself with his brother Caspar on the premises of the theatre, the project subsequently had to be abandoned.

While in the country, and after his return to Vienna, the great *Eroica* Symphony this year occupied much of his attention, and progressed far towards completion. The idea of this work was first suggested so far back as 1798, when Beethoven made the acquaintance of Bernadotte the French ambassador, and a musical amateur of some consideration. In the first instance, as is well known, Beethoven, fired with generous enthusiasm by the early exploits of the First Consul, inscribed the name of Napoleon upon the title-page—a name associated in his mind, at the time, with that republican cause to which (much to the prejudice of his interest at court) he was known to be so ardently devoted. As soon, however, as the news reached Vienna that his favourite had donned the Imperial purple, the composer tore up his title-page and stamped upon it in a frenzy of rage. His idol had fallen; but not the hero of his imagination, whose struggles, triumph, and death are celebrated in this most heroic of tone poems. By the magic of genius, the external event first selected for his subject matter had been gradually idealized and enlarged, and as the scope of his original intention widened, the theme, from being individual, grew to be representative of a type. The name of no single hero, therefore, appeared upon the new title-page—only *Sinfonia Eroica per festeggiare il sovvenire d'un grand' 'uomo.*

As compared with its two predecessors—produced in 1800 and 1803 respectively—this third Symphony was a new departure, and may be justly described as epoch-making, marking, as it did, the final abandonment by Beethoven of the influence of Mozart and Haydn which pervade, though always with a difference, his earlier works, and the more confident assertion of his own individuality. The *Eroica* was performed first in private during the winter of 1804 at the house of Prince Lobkowitz, to whom it was dedicated, but was not published before 1806.

Owing to a change in the administration of the Theatre *An der Wien*, and the transfer of the management from Schikaneder to Baron von Braun, the operatic scheme for the present fell through, and Beethoven once more shifted his quarters, this time to rooms in the Rothe Haus. In this new undertaking he was joined, most unfortunately, as the event proved, by his friend, Stephan Breuning; and the arrangement led to a painful episode in Beethoven's life—a quarrel with the old companion of his boyhood, who had so long stood towards him almost in the relation of a brother.

In the first instance the young men arranged to occupy two sets of rooms in the Rothe Haus, each with a separate domestic establishment. Eventually the idea —well described by Thayer as an "unfortunate economy" —occurred to them, that still closer comradeship, besides saving of money, might be attained by abandoning one suite and living together in the other. By omitting to give timely notice to the landlord, Beethoven found himself liable for both rooms. This led to hot words between himself and Breuning, and the rupture—thanks, evidently, in a great measure to the mischievous influence of Caspar—bid fair at one time to be permanent. Two letters written by Beethoven at the time to his friend Ries show how bitter were the feelings aroused by this affair. Angry, and ill in body and mind, Beethoven sought refuge first in Baden, and afterwards in his old quarters at Döbling. Breuning's conduct throughout was in keeping with his general habit of self-command and kindliness of character. Forgetting all grievances in his sympathy for the calamity which had befallen his sorely-tried friend, this is how he wrote to Wegeler, 13th November—

"You can form no idea how indescribable, how terrible, is the impression made upon him by his loss of hearing. Picture to yourself what must be his misery, with his excitable temperament, his habit of distrusting his best friends, and his frequent indecision. To sustain conversation with him is a positive exertion, and one can never be at ease; rarely indeed does his old true nature now allow itself to be seen."

It is satisfactory to know that before long a reconciliation was effected, and their old friendship re-established. Later on, another unhappy breach between Beethoven and Breuning, again brought about by Beethoven's hasty and suspicious temper, will have to be recorded.

While at Döbling this year, Beethoven was busy with the Grand Sonata in C, dedicated to Count Waldstein, and the smaller Sonata, Op. 54, in F. In connection with the last-named work, Ries, in a characteristic anecdote, describes a long country walk they took together, during which Beethoven uttered never a word, but was by no means silent; for he continued to hum to himself, and to beat the air with an accompaniment of extraordinary vocal sounds, representing, as he explained in answer to his companion's anxious inquiries, "the finale of a sonata." Arrived home, Beethoven, without stopping to take off his hat, ran immediately to the piano, and let loose the music with which his brain was teeming. He played for an hour; his pupil, the while, seated in a corner, listening and wondering.

Concerning his experiences of Beethoven as a teacher Ries has left somewhat conflicting accounts; sometimes describing him as seated at one end of the room while his pupil played at the other, and complaining that Beethoven seldom sat beside him at the piano for half an hour together; whereas on another occasion he testifies to the immense trouble the master would take to make him repeat over and over again passages that were not executed to his satisfaction; adding that "on such occasions the lesson would sometimes extend over two hours." In any case, Ferdinand, throughout his intimate association with the great composer, must have enjoyed opportunities for self-improvement of a kind to make him the envy of all young music students of that time. A plan was mooted for a concert tour, to be undertaken jointly by master and pupil, according to which Ries was to act as a sort of manager, attend to business details, and play his master's concertos and other works; Beethoven to conduct and extemporize. But this was never carried into effect.

Before his departure from Vienna, which took place the following year, Ries made his first appearance in public as Beethoven's acknowledged pupil, at the Augarten. On this occasion the Concerto in C minor was performed, and Ries introduced a cadence of his own. "Beethoven," he says in his *Notizen*, "conducted and turned the pages for me. I had urged him to compose a cadenza, but he told me to write one for myself. On the whole he was content with my composition, and made but few alterations. At the same time he told me to change one showy and exceedingly difficult passage, which he considered too risky. The more simple passage substituted was not to my taste, and I could not bring myself to play it in public. The crucial moment arrived. Beethoven seated himself quietly beside me; but as soon as I plunged boldly into the more difficult cadence, he gave his chair a violent push. The cadence, however, was a success, and Beethoven gave vent to his satisfaction by a 'Bravo!' which astonished the house."

The return of Schikaneder to the Theatre *An der Wien*, as manager under Baron von Braun, caused Beethoven again to give his attention to dramatic music; and 1805 was made memorable by the production of his first and only opera, *Fidelio*. The now well-known story of Leonora was founded upon a French libretto. It had been twice set to music in long-forgotten operas of Gaveaux and Paer; and *Leonora ossia l'amore conjugale,* by the last-named, had been performed at Dresden as recently as October in the previous year. Beethoven's noble conception of true womanhood finds expression in many passages of his letters, and it has been further proved by the honourable nature of his many attachments from youth upwards. To this feeling may be traced his selection of faithful wedded love for the theme of his first opera, and of the brave, devoted, self-sacrificing Leonora for his heroine. The prayer he once uttered—"O God! let me at last find her who was destined to be mine, and who shall strengthen me in virtue"—was never granted. But if, throughout his earthly pilgrimage, this ideal companionship was denied him, at least it shone upon him, radiant and etherealized, in the realm of his own poetical imaginings.

Beethoven had again taken up his lodging at the theatre. Some rooms also in Baron Pasqualati's house on the Mölk Bastion were kept at his disposal, and there he took refuge when specially anxious to pursue his work without fear of interruption from patrons, publishers, or friends. Amid the meadows and groves of Hetzendorf, whither he went in the month of June, he surrendered himself to the work of *Fidelio,* elaborating, extending, curtailing, and changing his musical ideas with that wonderful industry and incessant self-criticism to which his sketch-books bear testimony. Busy as he was, Beethoven found time to pay flying visits to Vienna, where Cherubini and his wife had lately arrived. Beethoven held the works of this composer in high esteem, and appreciated his companionship. Record exists of one visit to Sonnleithner's rooms, where he met both Cherubini and Vogler, "and they all played."

On Beethoven's return to the capital, the worries of rehearsal commenced with unusual severity. Composer and vocalists came into conflict—not an altogether unprecedented occurrence—and complaints of impossible passages and impossible high notes had to be frowned down or otherwise dealt with. The orchestra showed itself equally restive; and Beethoven, in those days, declared this opera of *Fidelio* to be "the most distressful business in the world." Unfortunately, distressful as it may have been in rehearsal, it proved still more so in performance.

A less propitious time for the production of an opera like *Fidelio* could hardly have been chosen. Vienna was then in a state of political ferment. On the 13th November the French army made their entry into the capital; the streets swarmed with troops, and Beethoven's former idol, Napoleon, was at Schönbrunn. All the leading members of Viennese society—the men of wealth and culture, to whose taste *Fidelio oder die eheliche liebe* would be likely to appeal—all Beethoven's patrons except the few among them who were also his intimate associates, had departed to their country seats or elsewhere. But less surprising than the failure of *Fidelio* was the fact that Beethoven's supporters should have consented to the production of such a work at such a time. And perhaps the most surprising thing of all was the acceptance as final of a verdict obtained under such conditions, after no more than four performances. After the first, which took place on the 20th November, a council of war was held at the house of Prince Lichnowsky, and, during a discussion of six hours' duration, various proposals for the curtailment of the work were made, and hotly opposed by the composer. Roeckel has given an interesting account of the scene. Far from joining in the general stampede, Lichnowsky was at his post, seated at the piano, score in hand. In a corner of the room, Clement accompanied on the violin; while Meyer and Roeckel did their best with the voice parts. And last, but by no means least, there was present the good, kindly princess, without whose intercession, as the narrator remarks, the labour of all the others would probably have been in vain. As it was, the opera was rehearsed to the end, and the composer's consent obtained to the withdrawal of three of the numbers. One little characteristic touch in Roeckel's recital is eminently in keeping with the impression one derives from other sources of Beethoven's impetuous but forgiving disposition. While the fight lasted, he tells us, the composer, according to his wont when any opposition was offered to his wishes, was ill-tempered and disagreeable. As soon, however, as all questions under discussion were settled, he was brimful of good-humour, and cracked jokes in his boisterous fashion, although the general verdict ran counter to his own opinion.

Nevertheless, the time was one of severe disappointment and annoyance for Beethoven. As usual in such cases, many of the minor critics, before covertly hostile, readily seized so tempting an opportunity for breaking into open abuse; and the composer, unfortunately, was then in no mood to treat their shafts with indifference. After three representations before audiences chiefly composed of French officers and soldiers, *Fidelio* was withdrawn. When the libretto had been improved by Stephan Breuning, and reduced from three to two acts, the opera was again performed, with a new overture, on March 29th, 1806. One more performance, on April 10th, brought its career to a close, as far as Vienna was concerned, for seven or eight years.

The fact that Beethoven wrote in all four different overtures for this single opera is one proof among many of his inexhaustible fancy and his immense capacity for work. It will be useful to set them forth in the order of their performance, without regard to the sequence of numbers by which they are generally known.

No. 2.—Played at the three first performances in Vienna, 20th, 21st, and 22nd November, 1805.

No. 3.—Played at Vienna, 29th March and 10th April, 1806.

No. 1.—Written for a proposed production of the opera at Prague, early in 1807, which did not take place.

No. 4.—Played at Vienna, 26th May, 1814.

There are more reasons than one for regretting the coldness with which the earlier performances of Beethoven's first opera were received in Vienna. At that time he showed a decided inclination for dramatic composition, and would very likely have pushed further in the same direction had not his ardour been damped at the very outset. But even while engrossed in this theatrical venture, he was at work also in other directions; and part of the Pianoforte Concerto in G and of the C minor Symphony, besides the two last of the famous String Quartets, Op. 59, dedicated to Count Rasoumoffsky, were composed in that year of excitement.

During the summer of 1806, the country, over-run by foreign troops, no longer offered the tranquil resting-place to which Beethoven had been accustomed. Invitations, therefore, from aristocratic friends were readily accepted; and he passed some months at the country seat of Count Brunswick—the brother of that Theresa of Brunswick whom some biographers have claimed to be the origin of the posthumous love-letters more generally supposed to have been addressed to Giulietta Guicciardi.

Later in the year, Beethoven paid a visit to Prince Lichnowsky in Silesia; and here occurred another of those regrettable scenes which were too often brought about by his irritability and offensive display of independence. Some French officers happened at the time to be quartered upon the prince, and the presence in the house of so eminent a *virtuoso* naturally whetted their curiosity. Beethoven was asked to play—always a dangerous request, as we know, to make in his case—and when, either for a freak, or incited by political animosity, he refused, the host pressed him, and jocularly threatened to lock him up. A turbulent scene ensued. The irate composer posted back to Vienna that same night, and on his return home seized a bust of his old friend the prince, and relieved his feelings by shivering it to atoms.

The comparative failure of *Fidelio* proved a severe disappointment to Beethoven in a pecuniary as well as in an artistic sense; but a liberally supported benefit concert in 1807, at which the new Symphony, No. 4, in B flat, was performed; a sale of copyrights made to Clementi, now head partner of a London music publishing firm, together with other profits resulting from an exceptionally productive period, removed, for the moment, all anxiety. As far as money matters were concerned, Beethoven at that time was inclined to regard the outlook as decidedly cheerful, and in May he wrote to Brunswick—"I can now hope, in a few years, to be in a position to maintain the true dignity of an artist."

It is believed that during this year Beethoven was occupied with both the Pastoral Symphony and the Symphony in C minor. In September, also, the Mass in C was produced at the chapel of Eisenstadt, under the auspices of Prince Esterhazy. From Beethoven's own words, when writing to the prince, there seems reason to suppose that the composer himself was not altogether content with this excursion into the field of ecclesiastial music. "Shall I tell you," he says, "that it is not without many misgivings that I shall send the Mass to you, who, I know, have been accustomed to hear the inimitable works of the great Haydn?" After the performance, something like a quarrel occurred between Beethoven and his old rival Hummel, who at that time filled the post of Capellmeister to Esterhazy.

Beethoven's "misgivings" were so far realized that Haydn's former patron was taken aback by a style of composition so different from what he had been accustomed to associate with Church music. His criticism was expressed in a form which might be freely translated into the vernacular by—"What on earth have you been doing *now?*" Unfortunately, the courtly Capellmeister happened to be within hearing, and made matters worse by what the composer, rightly or wrongly, supposed to be an approving laugh. Mortally offended, Beethoven left the palace, and for some time all intercourse ceased between him and Hummel.

The two court theatres were managed, during 1807, by an association of noblemen, with Lobkowitz at their head. We have further evidence of Beethoven's inclination at that time to pursue dramatic work, in his offer to contract for the supply of one grand opera and one operetta yearly, at a salary of 2400 florins, with benefit performances—a proposal, however, which was not accepted.

Meanwhile each year brought with it some memorable musical event—some work or works that would have sufficed to place their composer upon a pinnacle never before reached in the domain of instrumental music, even had they stood alone instead of being, as they were, but units in a stupendous catalogue of great achievements. Among such belonging to 1808 are the titanic C minor Symphony, which some persons are fond of regarding as a sort of musical apotheosis of will made victorious over fate by submission to its decrees, and the Choral Fantasia, interesting as a new departure destined hereafter to culminate in the Ninth Symphony.

And now musical amateurs of Vienna, who had long lived in the reflected glory of Beethoven's achievements, were startled into a sudden sense of indebtedness to their great tone-poet when it became known that Jerome Bonaparte, King of Westphalia, anxious to attach Beethoven to his court, had offered him the post of *Maître de Chapelle* at Cassel, with an annual salary, in addition to travelling expenses, of about £300. It was probably quite as far from Beethoven's own wish as from that of his friends, that the liberality of a foreign potentate should be allowed thus to eclipse his Austrian patrons. But the pension from the Elector had long since ceased, and with the exception of a small allowance from Prince Lichnowsky, Beethoven relied for support solely upon the money earned by his works. The moment, therefore, was in every sense a favourable one for urging his claim to some further allowance; and this opportune pressure from without was exploited to such good effect by Beethoven's friends, that in March 1809 the Archduke Rudolph, Prince Lobkowitz, and Prince Kinsky gave a joint undertaking to secure him 4000 florins, payable half-yearly—an allowance, it is true, of uncertain and fluctuating value; worth at the time it was granted a little over £200 (nominally £400), and unlikely to remain even at that figure in the immediate future. Eventually, indeed, owing to the rapid depreciation of the Austrian paper-money, the death and bankruptcy a few years afterwards of Prince Kinsky, and to other troubles connected with the affair, this well-meant arrangement resulted in more worry and disappointment for the composer than material benefit. Among the minor annoyances connected with it, was the necessity of sending to the executors of Prince Kinsky a certificate of his continued existence, which greatly exasperated Beethoven. He generally sent such documents through his friend Schindler; and one of them was couched in the following terms—

"*Certificate.*—The fish is alive.
"Vidi.
"PASTOR ROMUALDUS."

Ignaz Moscheles, who had recently lost his father, came to Vienna in 1809 to continue his musical studies; and no sooner had he arrived there than he was consumed with an ardent desire to see and become acquainted with Beethoven. This proved no easy matter; for except young Ries, Beethoven took no pupils, and his increasing deafness, and his frequent fits of despondency, rendered him ever more difficult of approach. At length fortune favoured the young student. One morning Moscheles happened to be standing in the shop of Artaria the publisher, when "some one," he writes, "entered with short, hasty steps; and with downcast eyes, as if wishing to pass unnoticed, walked straight through the circle of ladies and gentlemen, who were discussing business and musical matters, into the private office behind the shop. Artaria afterwards called me in and said, 'This is Beethoven'; and to the composer, 'This is the young man I was speaking to you about.' Beethoven nodded kindly, and said he had had a good account of me. He did not reply to a few stammered words of àdmiration, and seemed to wish to cut short the interview."

Moscheles's connection with Salieri, first as his pupil, and for three years as his deputy-assistant at the opera, gradually brought him into closer contact with the master; and later, at the suggestion of Artaria, the task was confided to him of preparing the pianoforte arrangement of *Fidelio*. His delight at this proposal was doubled by the conditions attached to it by Beethoven—viz. that he should see every number before it went to press. The long-sought chance of placing himself on terms of intimacy with the great man was thus put within his reach. But, owing to Beethoven's deafness, Moscheles did not derive from this intercourse all the pleasure and profit he had expected.

In 1809—a remarkable year in respect both of music composed and of music published—Beethoven first commenced his relations with the eminent publishing firm of Breitkopf and Härtel. Another publisher—a certain Thomson of Edinburgh—renewed a proposal which had remained in abeyance since 1806, that he should harmonize a number of national melodies. For Beethoven this must have been a mere matter of business; and again we have an instance of his untiring industry in the fact that, undeterred by his numerous more important occupations, he arranged over a course of years one hundred and sixty-four tunes, for which he was paid £200 in all.

This was a year also of immense political excitement in consequence of Napoleon's aggressive movements in

Italy, where his raids upon Tuscany and the States of the Church aroused general indignation. War was renewed in the spring, but with no happier results for Austria than had followed her previous efforts to arrest the progress of the French invader. The splendid German army, commanded by the Archduke Charles, was routed at Eckmühl on the 22nd of April; and on the 12th of May the French forces made a second entry into Vienna. During the bombardment the noise had a terror for the deaf musician, far removed from that personal cowardice vaguely insinuated in an account of the affair written, not by one of his enemies, but by a friend. Like many others among the non-fighting inhabitants, Beethoven took refuge in a cellar while the firing continued, and, dreading the effects of the explosions upon his sense of hearing—a dread which will be easily understood by those similarly afflicted—he endeavoured to lessen the effect of the vibrations with the aid of cushions. Two days later the Archduke left Vienna; and the first movement of the Sonata, Op. 81*a*, afterwards dedicated to him, contains the well-known *Les Adieux, L'Absence, et le Retour*. This title, therefore, unlike that of the *Moonlight* Sonata and some others, is not a publisher's addition, but a real title of occasion, furnished by the composer himself.

While the French, for the second time, were in possession of Vienna, the venerable Haydn lay on his deathbed, and on the 31st May he breathed his last. There were to be no more chance meetings, no more half-comical passages-of-arms between Haydn and his former pupil. In spite of such occasional friction, Beethoven, let it be said, held the master in sincere esteem, both as man and musician, to the end of his life.

In the May time of 1810, that strange, sprightly being, Bettina Brentano, came like a gleam of sunshine across Beethoven's path. Full of enthusiasm for the master's music, and eager to become personally acquainted with him, she went straight to his house one morning accompanied by her sister; and there and then made conquest of his heart. The sudden appearance in his lodgings of "Goethe's child," and the intimacy that was forthwith struck up between them, proved a source of new-found joy for that strange compound of roughness and sensibility. Beethoven sang for her, in his way, *Kennst du das Land?* walked home with her to Brentano's; arranged further meetings,—once more, in short, gave signs of that blissful predicament generally known as "love at first sight." Seeing, however, that Bettina was already betrothed to Count Arnim, this affection, in spite of the high-flown correspondence that passed between them, must have been recognized by him as hopeless from the very first. A description of Bettina, left by one of her contemporaries, renders intelligible the deep feeling she inspired in the inflammatory heart of the composer. "There was a strangeness," we are told, "about her whole appearance. With a small, delicate, and most symmetrical figure, pale clear complexion, interesting rather than strikingly handsome features, and a profusion of long black hair, she seemed the incarnation or indeed the original of *Mignon*. And her ways were as unconventional as her appearance When singing, one of her favourite seats was a writing-table, perched upon which 'she warbled like a cherub from the clouds.'" In marked contrast to the generality of German girls, she seldom condescended to feminine work; and visitors generally found her "comfortably squatting on a low footstool, or near the window, with a volume of Goethe in her lap." Impulsive and generous to a fault, she once, it is said, seized a roll of notes and gave half away without counting them to a person in distress.

The three famous letters from Beethoven, published years afterwards by Bettina, have long been a bone of contention for biographers. It is more than probable that the account given by the fascinating little woman herself of her interviews with the composer owe something to the colouring of a too vivid imagination. Such objectiou, indeed, amounts simply to a reasonable doubt whether the diary of a clever, highly-strung girl like Bettina would, in any case, be likely to be distinguished by strict historical accuracy. All unconsciously she revealed somewhat of the method adopted in her reminiscences, when she admitted that Beethoven, one morning, looking over her description of the previous day's proceedings, asked with an astonished air, "Did I really talk like this? I must have had a *raptus*." Though the three letters written by Beethoven may also have received embellishment at the hand of their romantic recipient, they may reasonably be credited with a substratum of truth. The last, dated from Toeplitz, 15th August, 1812, commences with an interesting reference to Goethe—

"It is indeed in the power of kings and princes to create professors and privy counsellors, and to bestow titles and decorations, but they cannot create great men. Spirits that assert their ascendancy over the common herd they cannot pretend to make; and thus they are compelled to respect them. When two such men as Goethe and myself come together, these fine people must be left to discover the meaning of the word 'great,' as this is understood by such as we.

"When returning home yesterday we met the whole Imperial family; we saw them coming in the distance. Goethe immediately dropped my arm, and stood aside. Say what I would to him, I could not get him to move a single step. I drew my hat lower down upon my head, buttoned up my greatcoat, and with arms folded pressed forward through the thickest of the crowd. A line was formed by princes and courtiers. Duke Rudolph raised his hat, the Empress bowing first. The great ones of the earth *know me!* To my inexpressible amusement, I noticed, when the procession passed, Goethe stood at the side, hat in hand, bending low. I took him to task for it pretty severely, and did not spare him. I brought up against him all his sins, especially those against you, dearest friend; for we had just been talking about you. Heavens! had I been permitted the intercourse that *he* has enjoyed, I should have produced far more great works."

Anything like a complete enumeration of the noble compositions that emanated from Beethoven's pen during the period of wonderful productiveness between 1804 and 1814, when his powers were at their height, together with an account of their characteristic features, would require a volume to itself. Besides many Pianoforte Sonatas of pre-eminent beauty—"Symphonies in miniature," as they have been called—including the D minor and the *Appasionata*, the record would embrace the opera of *Fidelio*, with its four overtures; the two Pianoforte Concertos in G and E flat; the one Violin Concerto; the First Mass; the overtures to *Coriolanus* (Collins's tragedy), to *King Stephen*, and the *Ruins of Athens;* the music to *Egmont;* the *Choral Fantasia;* the *Rasoumoffsky Quartets;* and many another notable work; lastly, those six Symphonies ranging from the third (*Eroica*) to the eighth, each of which has been rightly described as a musical event—a revelation of new possibilities in the realm of tone-poetry, possessing in some respects features unlike any to be found in works that had gone before, or in those that came after, even from the same pen. The illustration of Goethe's poem, *Calm Sea and Prosperous Voyage*, although not the earliest example of programme music, may be said, together with the Pastoral Symphony and other works, to have directed the attention of modern composers to the class of composition now known by that name.

The year 1810 is associated with another matrimonial project—the mysterious *Hierathspartie*, concerning which, and the object of it, there has been so much speculation. The fact that matters became sufficiently serious to cause Beethoven to write urgently for his baptismal certificate encourages a supposition that, whoever may have been the object of his choice, he was this time brought nearer to the brink of matrimony than on many similar occasions. Theresa of Brunswick has been mentioned as the possible heroine of the romance; but the whole affair remains enshrouded in mystery. Giulietta, as we know, had for some time been Countess

Gallenberg. According to Breuning the engagement was broken off three months afterwards. But in this, as in similar experiences, Beethoven escaped at least one of the consequences to which those who have passed through the fire of blighted love are not infrequently exposed. He never turned woman-hater. Two years later, when at Toeplitz, on the contrary, he became warmly enamoured of a charming, intellectual girl from Berlin—Amalie Sebalde; and a lock of hair cut by her from Beethoven's head is still in possession of the family. "Press the countess's hands for me," he wrote to Tiedge, "tenderly but respectfully. Give Amalie a loving kiss when no one is looking."

A great favourite with Beethoven—although the two had their quarrels—was the "fine pretty little woman," the Countess Erdödy; so described by Reichardt during her early married life, although she afterwards became a confirmed invalid. Another valued friend was "his dear Dorothea Cæcilia"—the talented Madame von Ertmann, who, again according to the testimony of Reichardt, ranked among the ablest contemporary exponents of Beethoven's music—a lady worthy of remembrance if only in association with a charming and pathetic anecdote. Visiting her a short time after the death of her son, Beethoven, conscious, as so many others have been, of the utter insufficiency of language to console on such occasions, went to the piano and said, "Let us talk only in tones!" "And he told me ALL," exclaimed Madame Ertmann, years afterwards when relating the occurrence. Here at least, it may be contended, music lost nothing in power and intensity by dissociation from the "spoken word."

A loan of 2300 florins obtained from his friends, the Brentanos, in 1812, suggests a far from satisfactory state of finances, and no doubt the depreciation of the Austrian paper-money, together with other difficulties connected with the pension from which at one time he had anticipated permanent and substantial assistance, was beginning to cause him considerable perplexity.

Spohr was at Vienna in 1812, and had the privilege of hearing Beethoven play during a rehearsal at the composer's house. But considering that the piano was very much out of tune—"which was of very little consequence to Beethoven, for he could not hear it"—and that the artist's deafness had left little trace of his once famous powers as a *virtuoso*, it is not surprising to learn that the experience afforded him no pleasure.

As his infirmity increased, Beethoven's pianoforte playing, both in public and private, became ever rarer. We find him still able, however, to extemporize at a concert given at Carlsbad for the benefit of sufferers in a fire at Baden. Another example of this willingness to co-operate in good works occurred at the beginning of the same year. In response to an application for assistance at a concert to be held at Gratz for the poor, he supplied four out of the eight numbers in the programme with compositions of his own, and declined to receive any payment.

Beethoven's intimacy with "Goethe's child" led, in due course, to an acquaintance with Goethe himself. This occurred at Toeplitz. Sooner or later such an approach would have been, in any case, inevitable. Evidences abound in Beethoven's letters and recorded conversation of the powerful influence exercised over his mind by the works of Goethe; and on Goethe's side there was a sincere recognition of the musician's surpassing genius and nobility of soul. But although the two strong natures had much in common, they had not everything; and on both sides there seems to have been a critical disposition which prevented the relations of mutual esteem at any time from ripening into brotherly friendship. Goethe's own description of the composer addressed to his friend Zelter gives us some idea of the nature of that limit. "I made acquaintance," he says, "with Beethoven in Toeplitz. His marvellous talent astounded me. But unfortunately he is an utterly untamed character. He is not indeed wrong in finding the world detestable. Still his finding it detestable does not make it any more enjoyable either to himself or to others." Perhaps, too, the poet did not retain a very gratifying recollection of a walk he once took with Beethoven in Vienna. He had been highly gratified by the frequent and respectful salutations of the passers-by, and these at length became so marked that he exclaimed, "Really I had no idea the people here knew me so well." "Oh!" the composer replied, with more regard for the truth than for his companion's feelings, "they are bowing to *me*, not to you." Beethoven's own account, in a letter to Bettina, of the two men's marked difference of demeanour when Duke Rudolph and the Empress passed by, and of the way in which Goethe was taken to task, has already been quoted.

As a matter of fact the composer seems to have soon passed out of Goethe's mind. Later, when Beethoven begged him in an humble letter to use his influence with Karl August in connection with the Mass, the poet did not even trouble himself to send a reply.

Of the many doctors consulted by Beethoven in these years, none inspired him with greater confidence than Dr. Malfatti; although with him, as with most of the others, a quarrel presently ensued. The physician's two charming daughters, Theresa and Anna, were immense favourites with him. In one of his letters to Gleichenstein, who married the younger sister in 1811, he says, "My greetings to all who are dear to you and to me. How gladly would I add—to whom we are dear ? ? ? ? These marks of interrogation at least become me." Of the society *belle*, Theresa, he writes, she is "volatile, and takes everything in life lightly, but with keen perception of all that is beautiful and good, and a great talent for music."

By Malfatti's advice Beethoven tried the baths of Bohemia in 1812, before making his excursion to Toeplitz. Later in the same year he was back in his old rooms at Vienna, in Pasqualati's house on the Mölk Bastion.

Beethoven's frequent changes of lodgings may be attributed partly to that restless sensitiveness to external influences which turned inconveniences, more or less trivial in themselves, into serious obstacles to work; partly, also, to his longing for privacy, and the ever-increasing difficulty of obtaining it. Sometimes there was not enough sunshine in his room; sometimes the quality of the drinking water was unsatisfactory, or he did not like the landlord. Schindler says it was no uncommon thing for Beethoven to have three or four lodgings on his hands—and thus three or four rents to pay—at the same time. Once, when some rooms were placed at his disposal in the residence of Baron Ponay, a novel grievance awaited him. The ceremonious greetings of his host, each time they met in the fine park by which the villa was surrounded, and the necessity of returning them, so greatly tried his patience that his stay in those seemingly desirable quarters was limited to a few days.

Of the hopeless disorder of the rooms themselves—before a good-natured friend came to the rescue—both Oulibischeff and Seyfried have given graphic descriptions. "Books and music were scattered all about the room; in one place the remains of a cold snack; in another a wine-bottle; on the desk a hasty sketch of a new quartet; near it the fragment of breakfast; on the piano some scrawled pages containing a glorious symphony in embryo; proofs waiting for correction and business letters strewing the floor. Once an important paper was not to be found—not a sketch nor a loose sheet—nothing less than a thick, clearly copied score from the Mass in D. It was found at last, but where do you think? In the kitchen, wrapped round something to eat."

Beethoven made one desperate attempt to settle the "servant question" by dismissing them all, housekeeper included, and taking the household duties upon his own shoulders. According to one account he even invited some friends to a dinner cooked by himself; "but the maestro soon discovered that composing and cooking were different things, and the injured cook was speedily reinstated." The story, it should be added, has been contradicted by Schindler. Something like order was at last introduced into this chaotic domicile by good Frau Babette Streicher, the wife of a well-known instrument-maker. In the absence of a mistress of the household, this helpful, kindly woman set to work with much needed energy and with highly satisfactory results; engaging and keeping a watch over servants, rehabilitating the wardrobe, and standing generally between the composer and the minor domestic worries of life.

Winter and summer Beethoven rose at daybreak, when he immediately seated himself at his writing-table, and continued writing until his usual dinner-time of two or three o'clock. His labours were broken by occasional excursions into the open air, but never without a note-book in which to jot down whatever fresh ideas might occur during his rambles. The habit of going out suddenly, and as unexpectedly returning, was practised at all seasons of the year, just as the whim happened to seize him. "Cold or heat," says Schindler, "rain or sunshine, were all alike to him. In the autumn he used to return to town as though he had been sharing the daily toil of the reapers and gleaners. Winter restored his somewhat yellow complexion."

In connection with Beethoven's fondness for water, the same biographer has described how, during moments of inspiration, he would rush to the washing-basin and empty several jugs over his hands, singing and shouting the while according to his favourite custom; and how at length the neighbours below were compelled to complain of the wet that trickled through their ceiling.

He loved the twilight. Generally he chose that hour for improvising—sometimes on the piano, sometimes on the violin or viola, which were always kept ready for him. Later in life, when his deafness had become serious, there was a wide difference between the intention and the sounds he actually produced upon bow instruments, and the effect was described as painful to hear.

Besides consulting numerous doctors Beethoven made several attempts to alleviate his deafness, if it could not be cured; and at one time his hopes were greatly raised by the promise from Maelzel—best known as the inventor of the metronome—of a new sound-conductor and sundry similar appliances to be manufactured expressly for him. These instruments, when finished, proved of doubtful value, and in the following year the connection led to many troubles.

Meanwhile, in recognition of his services, Beethoven composed for Maelzel a military piece to be performed on a sort of mechanical trumpet, which was about to be introduced into England, called the "Panharmonicon." This work, which was admittedly unworthy of Beethoven's powers, was called *The Battle of Vittoria*, in commemoration of the great defeat sustained by the French at that place; and it was afterwards arranged for orchestra, and played at a concert in December 1813, for the benefit of the soldiers wounded at Hanau.

Thanks to political enthusiasm and to a good performance of the seventh Symphony—also included in the programme—the concert was an immense success. Beethoven himself conducted in spite of his deafness; adapting his beat to the movements of Schuppanzigh's bow. In a letter of thanks afterwards addressed to the performers, he described this concert as "an unprecedented assembly of eminent artists, each inspired by the desire to achieve something by his art for the good of the Fatherland, and all working together unanimously, accepting subordinate positions regardless of precedent, for the sake of the general success. The direction of the whole," he goes on to say, "was undertaken by me simply because the music happened to be my composition. Had it been another's I would willingly, like Herr Hummel, have placed myself at the great drum. For our only feelings were those of pure love to the Fatherland, and the joyful dedication of our powers to the cause of those who have sacrificed so much for us."

On this occasion Spohr, for the first time, had an opportunity of seeing Beethoven conduct in public. "Although I had been warned beforehand," he says, "the whole thing greatly astonished me. Beethoven had accustomed himself to indicate to the orchestra the marks of expression by all sorts of extraordinary movements. Whenever a *sforzando* occurred he would vehemently open both arms, which had before been folded. For a *piano* he bent down, and the softer it was to be the lower he stooped. For a *crescendo* he drew himself ever higher and higher, till at the arrival of the *forte* he gave a leap into the air; he would also scream out, without knowing it, in order to emphasize an increase of the *forte*."

In spite of its inferiority as a composition, the Battle Symphony was equally successful with the English public, when produced at Drury Lane in the following year. Some time before the performance a copy of the work had been sent to the Prince Regent; but, greatly to the composer's chagrin, it was never even acknowledged.

Later a serious quarrel arose between Beethoven and Maelzel; and although different complexions have been put upon the affair by the partisans of either side, it does not seem to have been disputed that Maelzel was travelling about with a garbled version of the piece; so that whether or not he had actually purchased it, as he asserted, the indignation of the composer is not very surprising. Matters were further complicated and ill-feeling intensified by a misunderstanding with regard to a certain money transaction; Maelzel declaring that he had paid £25 to Beethoven for the copyright of the work, while Beethoven, on the other hand, maintaine that this was only a loan. So hot did the controversy grow that Beethoven commenced an action at law. A partial reconciliation was afterwards effected, but not before many hard words had been exchanged and much distress of mind entailed upon the composer.

Early in 1814 a young man called upon Beethoven with a letter from the violinist Schuppanzigh. The name of the visitor was Anton Schindler. Soon this casual acquaintance ripened into close intimacy; and, five years later, Schindler was established in the master's house as a kind of secretary and general assistant. This friendship was broken by a quarrel in which Beethoven's temper did not, it must be confessed, show itself to advantage, and the separation continued until a short time before his death, when the devoted secretary resumed his old position, and remained with the master till the end. When Breuning died Beethoven's papers came into the hands of Schindler, and with the aid of these and of his own personal recollections, the latter was enabled to give to the world the well-known biographical work with which his name is chiefly associated. The appearance of the book was greeted with plentiful abuse in some quarters, but time has brought with it a juster estimate of Schindler's labours, and the verdict of later and less biased criticism has been favourable, on the whole, to his accuracy of statement and soundness of judgment.

The memorable revival in 1814 of the opera *Fidelio* has an interesting chronicler in Friedrich Treitschke, who was manager and librettist of the two Imperial theatres in Vienna, and in that dual capacity rendered much valuable assistance towards the revision of the book. According to Treitschke's account, the attention of the then superintendents of the two opera-houses, Saal, Vogl, and Weinmüller, was first drawn to the long-neglected work in consequence of an absolute lack of worthy new compositions of the German school—a fact scarcely to be wondered at in view of the sort of encouragement that had been accorded to Beethoven's operatic masterpiece for years past; and meanwhile the latest French operas had so deteriorated in quality and declined in popularity, that "the actors had not the courage to throw themselves into the Italian works as mere singers, as they suicidally did a few years later."

In these circumstances Beethoven was applied to for the loan of *Fidelio*, to which he disinterestedly consented, on the understanding that certain alterations should be made, and for this purpose the services of Treitschke were called in. During their conference on the subject of the libretto, Treitschke showed proof of true dramatic feeling by objecting to an aria it was proposed to give to Florestan. "I pointed out that a man almost dead with hunger could not possibly sing *bravura*. The difficulty, however, was satisfactorily evaded by some appropriate lines of the poet, descriptive of the last flickering of the vital flame before it is extinguished, beginning—

"Und spür' ich nicht linde, sanft säuselnde Luft."

"What I am about to relate," wrote Treitschke in the musical annual *Orpheus*, "will ever live in my memory. Beethoven came to me at about seven in the evening. After we had discussed other matters, he asked how was the aria getting on? It was just ready. I handed it to him. He read it, walked up and down the room, murmuring and humming, which were his usual substitute for singing, and then threw open the piano. My wife had often vainly asked him to play; but now, he placed the text before him, and began a wonderful fantasia, which, unfortunately, there was no magic pen to rescue from oblivion. He seemed to conjure from it the motive of the aria. Hours passed, but still Beethoven played on. Our supper, which he was to share, was brought in; but he would not be disturbed. When quite late he embraced me, and, excusing himself from the meal, hurried home. The next day the music was ready."

The book was finished towards the end of March, and Beethoven thus acknowledged the copy that was sent to him.

"DEAR GOOD TREITSCHKE,—I have read your improved version with great pleasure. It has determined me to rebuild the ruins of an old castle.

"Your friend,

"BEETHOVEN."

The work, however, progressed slowly, and, as the composer remarked to his useful friend, there was a great deal of difference between working from cool reflection and abandoning one's self to inspiration.

The performance took place at the Kärnthnerthor on the 23rd of May. A new overture had been promised for the grand rehearsal on the day before; but Beethoven did not put in an appearance. "After waiting a long time," says Treitschke, "I went to fetch him. He was in bed fast asleep, a goblet of wine with a biscuit in it beside him, and the sheets of the overture scattered over the bed and floor. The exhausted lamp showed that he had been working far into the night." In fact it was not until the 26th May that this new overture (in E), now distinguished from the others by the title of Overture to *Fidelio*, was included in the performance.

The preparation of the pianoforte score of this opera by Moscheles, under Beethoven's direction, was the means of bringing the two into frequent communication, and Moscheles, who visited his rooms at all hours, has illustrated the composer's absence of mind by a characteristic anecdote. "I went early to Beethoven one morning, and found him still in bed. As it happened, he was in remarkably good spirits; jumped up and placed himself close to the window, so that he might be better able to examine the pieces. Of course a crowd of boys collected in the street underneath. 'What do the confounded youngsters want?' he exclaimed at last. I pointed smiling to his own figure. 'Yes, yes; you are right,' he cried, and quickly threw on a dressing-gown."

On another occasion Moscheles, not finding Beethoven in his lodgings, left his instalment of work upon the table, and wrote under it, "Finis, with God's help." Shortly afterwards he received it back from Beethoven with the additional words, "O man, help thyself!"

Beethoven's old friend, Prince Lichnowsky, was not spared to witness the successful revival of the opera in the first production of which he had so actively interested himself. One of the sorrowful events for Beethoven in 1814 was the death of his kind and generous patron. Lichnowsky died shortly before what may be called the culminating social triumph of Beethoven's life, when Vienna, crowded with kings, princes, and ambassadors, drawn thither by the great Congress, took pride in doing honour to the gifted musician whose principal life-work had been carried on in her midst.

The occasion, both socially and politically, was a favourable one for such a purpose. At the invitation of the municipality Beethoven composed specially a Cantata in celebration of the event, entitled *Der Glorreiche Augenblick*, which, like his previous work deriving its inspiration from a political motive, was altogether unworthy of his fame. Like its predecessor, also, it proved immensely successful; and its production was made the occasion of a concert which has become historical. The two halls of the Redouten-Saal, placed at his disposal by the Government, were crowded with an audience of some six thousand persons, including a galaxy of royal and distinguished visitors, and the enthusiasm was immense. After this, honours crowded thickly upon him. London, Paris, Stockholm, and Amsterdam created him honorary members of their respective Academies; and—a distinction he prized above all—Vienna presented him with the freedom of the city. During this year Beethoven, in better health and spirits than he had known for some time, threw off for a time his habits of a recluse, and allowed himself to be lionized and fêted in the drawing-rooms of the greatest in the land. In the house of his illustrious pupil the Archduke Rudolph, he was presented to the Empress Elizabeth of Russia. Their conversation was unconstrained and cordial; and before leaving Vienna the Empress presented him with two thousand ducats, the composer, in return, dedicating to her the Polonaise in C, Op. 89. Other presents, it may be inferred, were made to him by various great personages; for his financial position was so far improved by the year's transactions that, from being a borrower, he became an investor in shares of the Bank of Austria.

These gay times for Vienna were brought to a sudden termination when the news arrived of Napoleon's escape from Elba, and of his landing near Frejus on the 1st of March, 1815. Amid the general consternation Beethoven had anxieties on his own account. The Kinsky lawsuit dragged its course slowly along, much to the hindrance of composition, as is evident from letters to his lawyer written during that period. Soon too the sky, which had brightened for a season, was clouded in another quarter; and those domestic and business worries, which were fated to increase as time went on, already began to throw their shadows before them. The mischievous influence of his two brothers, in whom, despite frequent warnings from observant outsiders, Beethoven continued to repose unbounded confidence, at least contributed to another misfortune—a second quarrel with the good, faithful Stephan Breuning. The original cause of this untoward event was one of the warnings referred to. Breuning, at the instigation of some person who had observed with not unnatural suspicion the almost unlimited control assumed over Beethoven's affairs by his money-loving brother Carl, had undertaken the delicate duty of dropping a timely hint. Ever combative where the good faith of his relations was called in question, Beethoven, instead of appreciating Breuning's friendly intention, reported to Caspar not only the conversation, but also the informant's name. A quarrel with Caspar, as Breuning soon discovered, meant also a quarrel with Beethoven himself. High words ensued all round, and Caspar, as usual, fanned the flame. The affair ended in a separation between Beethoven and Breuning which lasted for several years. Thus two painful blanks were left in Beethoven's life by the removal of two of his truest friends, in one case by death, and in the other by estrangement. How much he suffered during this estrangement, and how sincerely he repented his hasty conduct, when his eyes were at length opened to the true state of the case—all this is feelingly expressed in a letter to Stephan, undated, but placed by Schindler in 1826, in which he encloses a miniature of himself by Horneman.

Attempts have been made to soften the many unfavourable comments that have been provoked by the conduct of Johann and Caspar Beethoven towards their brother. Though the evil they wrought may have been exaggerated, there is ample evidence that they interfered, in many cases, between him and his friends with most unfortunate results. And in another matter, also, their character does not come out quite clear. Beethoven, though careless, was the reverse of an extravagant man, and it is difficult to believe that the payments he obtained for his compositions—respectable prices for those days—together with the numerous presents of wealthy patrons received from first to last, would not have sufficed, if fairly dealt with, to preserve him during his last years from sordid care. The fact that Johann, the whilom apothecary, was living, meanwhile, in comparative affluence on a landed estate of his own, is also not without its significance.

In November 1815 Caspar died. He left to Ludvig

a legacy so disastrous in its consequences, that it throws into shade whatever evil he may have done him during life. From the day when Beethoven accepted the guardianship of young Carl—Caspar's son —a new sorrow was imported into his life. Henceforth the wealth of affection which dwelt in the heart of this rugged, single-hearted man—ever yearning for home ties and ever disappointed—was centred upon his new and, as he unhappily proved, unworthy charge. Scamp as Carl undoubtedly was, one is almost inclined to commiserate the terribly severe retribution which has been meted out to him by posterity. The irreparable evil wrought by him in the life of a great man has caused his insignificant personality to be singled out for opprobium from among other young men as bad or worse than himself, and has conferred upon him a place in history it is impossible to ignore; so that "Beethoven's worthless nephew" must ever figure prominently in any record of this last and saddest period of Beethoven's career.

The troubles connected with this ill-starred guardianship commenced immediately. Carl was between eight and nine years old when his father died; and Beethoven's first anxiety was to separate the boy from his mother, whom he believed to be a person of objectionable character. Not unnaturally, "The Queen of Night," as Beethoven used to call his sister-in-law, resented this attempt to ignore her maternal rights, and much bitterness and recrimination, and a lawsuit of four years' standing, followed. When Beethoven carried his cause to the Landrechts' Court—a Court open to none but appellants of noble family—his advocate made the singular mistake of citing the Dutch prefix of *Van* to his name, as a proof of aristocratic lineage. The composer's argument was of a less technical kind. "My nobility is *here* and *here*," he said, pointing alternately to head and heart. To his disgust this plea was not admitted as conclusive, and the case was retried in the Lower Court, and decided against him. But there still remained the High Court of Appeal; and from this tribunal Beethoven succeeded in obtaining a reversal of the former verdict. It was not until January 1820 that Carl was finally removed from surroundings which could not fail—as was still more clearly shown in the course of these legal proceedings—to be injurious to his future. The purely benevolent motives by which Beethoven was actuated in thus leaving no stone unturned to gain his end, stand out clearly in one of the earlier appeals, and were sufficiently proved by his subsequent conduct.

Unhappy as were the consequences of Beethoven's intense longing for a home of his own, and of his attempt to establish one for his adopted nephew—in default of those closer ties which were never to be his—the spectacle, nevertheless, of a composer, so utterly unfitted for practical affairs, seriously setting himself to master the mysteries of domestic economy, is not without its humorous side. Before embarking in this venturesome enterprise, and in order to fortify himself with at least some elementary knowledge of the subject, he formulated his perplexities in the following queries, addressed to a friend whom he may be supposed to have regarded as an expert in such matters:—

"1. What is the proper allowance, both in regard to quality and quantity, for the dinner and supper of two servants?

"2. How often ought one to give them meat? Should they have it both at dinner and supper?

"3. Do the servants take their meals off the food cooked for their master, or should some be cooked especially for them?

"4. How many pounds of butcher's meat are allowed for three persons?"

In 1816 yet another blank was left in the circle of Beethoven's friends by the death of Prince Lobkowitz; this event still further reduced the yearly pension, and an unsuccessful attempt to enforce by legal proceedings a continuance of the share contributed by Lobkowitz during his lifetime added to the worries which now gathered around the composer. For now the financial outlook again became gloomy. Some small relief was forthcoming from the sale to the Philharmonic Society, through Mr. Neate, of the MS. Overtures, *The Ruins of Athens*, and *King Stephen;* and early the following year a gratifying incident awaited him in the presentation of a grand pianoforte, forwarded from London by the well-known firm of Broadwood—a gift which has sometimes, but without confirmatory evidence, been attributed to the London Philharmonic Society. A proposal that Beethoven should pay a visit to London with two MS. Symphonies to be purchased by the Society, was also the subject of negotiations through

Ries at about this time, but owing to various causes came to nothing.

To the appointment in 1818 of his friend and pupil, the Archduke Rudolph, to the Archbishopric of Olmütz, the world owes a work characterized by Beethoven as the crowning achievement of his life. The work in question—the sublime *Missa Solennis*—was undertaken with a view to its performance on the Archduke's instalment, fixed for 20th March, 1820, but was not completed until two years after. It was composed under conditions of such excitement and utter self-absorption as may be well believed to have shut out, for the time, all consciousness of external troubles. As his companion Schindler tells us, Beethoven was as one actually "possessed"; and from the moment he threw his energies into this colossal undertaking his whole nature seemed to change—meals forgotten, appointments disregarded, long silent wanderings through the still fir forests of Baden, utter neglect of household matters; in short, a *raptus* transcending any similar condition witnessed by his old friend, Madame Breuning, in the early days. Once, when Schindler and a companion called upon him, they found the door closed, and from the room within an uproar reached their ears of "singing, howling, stamping." The "almost horrible" scene was enacted at four o'clock in the afternoon; and when Beethoven at length opened the door to his astonished visitors, his face bore traces of some strange and terrible struggle. "A pretty state of affairs here," he said; "everybody has left. I have not eaten a morsel since midday yesterday"—the fact being that he had worked the evening before until after midnight, and left his food untouched; while the servants, finding their attentions unnoticed, and regarding the proceedings, perhaps, as somewhat "uncanny," had forsaken the house. The composer's pale and famished appearance, and the disordered state of the room, must have presented an appearance of abject misery. Nevertheless, it is easy to believe that in the joy of artistic creation he was ready at such moments to pity the wealthiest and most illustrious of his patrons.

But amid all this work, what had now come to be the dominant purpose of his life—the accumulation of money for his scapegrace nephew—was never lost sight of. The Mass was completed, and a copy offered to all the principal courts of Europe for the sum of fifty ducats. When the King of Prussia suggested, through his ambassador, that perhaps a decoration might be more welcome than money, the composer promptly replied, "Fifty ducats."

In 1822 a young actress, then only seventeen, and presenting, according to Weber's description, "a miserable appearance," made her *début* at Vienna in the opera of *Fidelio*. Friends had openly expressed their opinion that her slightness of physique would prove an insurmountable barrier to success—and she was rendered additionally nervous by the presence in the orchestra, sitting behind the bandmaster Umlauf, of Beethoven himself, "so closely enveloped in his cloak that his eyes alone were visible." The young *bénéficiaire's* heart may well have quaked as she stepped upon the stage to challenge so critical an audience; but she left it that night the acknowledged ideal Leonora. This was the celebrated Wilhelmine Schröder Devrient, who threw into the part of the devoted wife a dramatic intensity that afterwards gained for her European reputation. After the fall of the curtain the formidable Beethoven advanced with smiles and thanks, and promises to compose a new opera expressly for her. But the promise was never to be fulfilled.

The wonderful list of Pianoforte Sonatas was brought to a worthy close by that in E major, Op. 109—written while the composer was still immersed in the great Mass—and by the Sonatas in A flat major and C minor, bearing the dates, respectively, of 25th Dec. 1821, and 13th Jan. 1822. And now followed also a crowning achievement in the department of orchestral music. So far back as 1812, vague projects of the Ninth Symphony had existed in the composer's mind, and foreshadowings of it, as has been seen, had already appeared in the Choral Fantasia. Traces of the gradual process by which the scheme grew and was elaborated until it took its final shape, are found in the sketch-books, which show, among other things, that the adoption of the *Ode to Joy* as a text for the vocal part in the finale was a later thought, although mention of an intention to treat musically Schiller's *Freude*, "and that verse by verse," occurred, as we have seen in a letter from Bonn to the poet's sister, dated so far back as 1793.

Many attempts have been made to describe the profound impression invariably produced by an adequate performance of this wondrous Ninth Symphony—to convey in words some notion of its power, its beauty, and its mystery. Attempts of this kind can never be more than partially successful, for the simple reason that much in the work is untranslatable outside the musical language to which it belongs. Here, however, if anywhere, the claim put forward for music as a moral and spiritualizing influence will have to be conceded. Beethoven had travelled far. From a height never attained before or since in the domain of symphonic music, his voice reached the world, charged with a message not comprehended by all, though all were able to recognize in it the utterances of a soul that had known how "to suffer and be strong." An assumption has been favoured in some quarters that Beethoven, when he introduced the *Ode to Joy* in the last movement, intended to mark certain limits beyond which musical expression, unaided by the spoken word, was unable to go. The writer, for one, is unable to discern in so simple an innovation any such announcement—or, indeed, any announcement at all; and the fact is worthy of remark that Beethoven immediately afterwards is seen engaged at his favourite work of quartet writing. For the rest, it is easy enough, without indulging in fanciful theory, to believe that the greatest of musico-dramatists who came after, found suggestion and inspiration in the heritage bequeathed by the greatest of symphonists; for of the works of Beethoven, as of all works of true genius, it may be said, in the words of an eloquent writer,[1] "they have an assimilative power, and as man changes they disclose

[1] *Guesses at Truth.*

new features and aspects, and ever look him in the face with the reflection of his own image, and speak to him with the voice of his own heart."

Much has been said and written on the subject of Beethoven's "three manners." When comparing the earliest with the latest works of a creative artist who once wrote, "the boundary-line does not exist of which it can be said to talent when united to industry, 'thus far shalt thou go, and no farther,'" a wide gulf in respect of style would be naturally looked for. Such marked difference, in fact, is found to exist between Beethoven's Ninth and last Symphony and his first produced more than twenty years before. As with all changes brought about by a process of natural growth, it is no more possible to fix the exact boundary lines separating the *Trois Styles* discussed in Herr von Lenz's well-known book, than it would be to indicate the precise points of departure of those seven ages of man so graphically depicted by the "melancholy Jacques." The form, the very dialect, employed by composers with whose fame the world was ringing in the days of Beethoven's youth, naturally supplied models for those earlier works that have been grouped together as representing the "first style"—works often redolent of Haydn and Mozart, but showing evidence in nearly every case of an originality that was destined soon to lead instead of follow. Even here, therefore, anticipations of that splendid array of compositions conveniently assigned to the "second style" are not infrequently to be found.

To the second period—a period of matured power

and comparative prosperity—the world owes a succession of masterpieces, each revealing in some new light the richness of an imagination as inexhaustible as it was many-sided. It was during this period that the forms transmitted to Beethoven by his predecessors soon ceased to be trammels; that while extending and ennobling them, he showed how possible it is to be original, to be intense, to be startling even, without violating, in any essential particulars, the comely shapeliness of the sonata form. While doing this he had, of course, to run the gauntlet, at each successive step, of that class of critics with whom the word "romanticism" was a term of reproach; and who forgot, like many of their successors, that the "romanticism" of one generation is often the "classicism" of the next. Fétis has made some pertinent remarks upon one innovation in Beethoven's music, which at once gave to it a distinctive character—the spontaneity of the episodes "by means of which he suspends the interest excited, while substituting another as striking as it is unexpected. This is an art peculiar to himself. In appearance foreign to the idea which precedes them, these episodes in the first place arrest attention by their originality. Afterwards, when the effect of surprise begins to wear off, he knows how to treat them as an integral portion of his plan, thus showing variety to be dependent upon unity."

But, as we have seen, there was still more to follow—the deep poetry, the almost mystic utterances of that Third Style, among which are included the later Pianoforte Sonatas and Quartets (to be hereafter referred to), the Mass, and the Ninth Symphony. A tenth symphony still more choral in character was also in contemplation, the first movement of which was to be an *andante cantique*, in the old modes, standing either by itself or leading into a fugue, and in which the voices were either to enter early, or else in the last movement after the repetition of the *adagio*.

In 1823 we read of further operatic projects; of the acceptance of *Melusina* by Grillparzer, and of a request from Count Bruhl that he would write a German opera for the Berlin theatre; but owing to the difficulty of finding a plot exactly suited to the composer's fancy, and to various other obstacles, all these intentions remained unfulfilled. In the same year he had a cordial interview with Weber, who had come to Vienna for the production of *Euryanthe*.

And now, musical taste in Vienna underwent a change that not only militated against Beethoven's material interests, but also deeply wounded his feelings as an artist. Rossini entered upon the field, and with his graceful Italian melodies fairly won over the ear of the public. There is nothing very surprising in the fact that amateurs in Vienna, like the rest of the world, should have yielded to the charm of tuneful gifts which, be it remembered, came upon them, at that time, as something fresh and in its way original. Less easy is it to understand how a society, supposed to have been thoroughly imbued with the spirit of Beethoven's masterpieces, should have shown itself so wholly satisfied with the comparatively trivial school represented by the southern singer as to turn away with sudden indifference from the higher fare upon which it had been nurtured for years. True, the old personal affection borne by the Viennese for their great composer still remained. The well-known figure of the deaf man as he paced the streets, or stood, as he was fond of doing, before shop-windows, double eyeglass in hand, taking stock of their contents, was still an object of mingled curiosity and reverence for the passers-by. The fact nevertheless remains, that the public, who had hitherto followed his achievements with enthusiasm, were now, so to say, left behind—wondering at rather than intelligently appreciating the onward advance of his profound and original genius; so that Beethoven now began to experience, at least in some measure, the disappointments and humiliations incidental to the lot of a "musician of the future."

Not only the old friends who still remained among the faithful, but many others occupying a more or less conspicuous position in the musical community, were roused to something like alarm, when it became known that Beethoven, in his chagrin at finding himself thus supplanted by "a mere scene-painter," as he called Rossini, entertained serious thoughts of producing the Mass and the new Symphony in Berlin. To slight Beethoven's music was one thing; but the bare thought of surrendering him to another capital both jarred upon their feelings and hurt their pride. An earnest remonstrance was drawn out, bearing signatures that could hardly fail to have weight with the composer, and arrangements were at length concluded for the performance of the two works at a grand concert, for which the Theatre *An der Wien*, in the first instance, was selected.

But soon fresh difficulties arose. Beethoven, more than ever suspicious of the machinations of "enemies," by whom he believed himself to be surrounded, firmly resisted the high terms demanded for the use of the house; and there seemed every chance, at one time, of the scheme falling through. In accordance with a little plot, suggested by Schindler to Count Moritz Lichnowsky and Schuppanzigh, the three friends met, as if by accident, at Beethoven's rooms, and after much trouble persuaded him to sign the required agreement. Their success, however, was of short duration; for no sooner had the three conspirators left his house than suspicions of foul play flashed anew into Beethoven's mind. The result was the early receipt of the three following missives:—

"To Count Moritz Lichnowsky,—I despise duplicity. Let me have no more of your visits. The Academy[1] will not take place.

"Beethoven."

"To Herr Schuppanzigh,—Let me see you no more. I shall give no concert.

"Beethoven."

"To Herr Schindler,—Do not come near me again until I send for you.

"Beethoven."

The concert nevertheless took place on 7th May, 1824,

[1] Concert.

at the Kärnthnerthor Theatre—the house ultimately decided upon—and parts of the Mass and the overture *Weihe des Hauses* were performed, together with the Ninth Symphony. Already, during the production of *Fidelio*, Beethoven had shown but scant mercy to the singers; and now a similar disposition to over-rate the capacities of the human voice, often observable among habitual composers for the orchestra, brought him into conflict with Sontag and Mademoiselle Ungher. When Mademoiselle Ungher called him the tyrant of singers, he retorted, with equal justness on his side, that they had all been spoilt for music such as his by the modern Italian style of singing. "But *this* passage," pleaded Sontag, pointing to some high notes in the vocal quartet of the Symphony—"could it not possibly be altered?" Mademoiselle Ungher chimed in with a similar appeal in regard to her own part; but the only answer was an emphatic refusal. "For heaven's sake, then," said Sontag, like the true artist and amiable creature she was, "let us work away at it again!"

Artistically the concert was a great success, but financially—in spite of a house crowded in every part by an audience eager to catch a sight of the world-famous musician, and to hear the two newest works from his pen—a great disappointment. One man alone was unconscious of the thunders of applause which followed the performance. This was Beethoven himself. "He continued standing with his back to the audience and *beating time* till Fraulein Ungher, who had sung the contralto part, turned him, or induced him to turn round and face the people, who were clapping their hands and giving way to the greatest demonstration of applause."[1] It is easy to believe the statement of one who was present on that occasion—that when the deaf musician bent his head in acknowledgment, many an eye among the faces he so calmly confronted was dim with tears.

It was his last public triumph. Expenses had been heavy, and receipts the reverse of satisfactory; for regular box-holders had entered free, and the payment usually contributed by the court on the occasion of a benefit was, for some reason, withheld. After deducting all disbursements, the net profit resulting from one of the most memorable concerts on record was under £40. Schindler describes the painful effect produced upon the already overstrung nerves of Beethoven when the news of this comparative disaster was first communicated to him. "He broke down altogether. We took him and laid him upon the sofa. He asked neither for food nor for anything else. He uttered no word. At length, when we noticed his eyes gently close in sleep, we left him. In this position, and still dressed in the green dress-coat he wore at the concert, his servant found him the next morning."

As for the concert that followed, it was a total failure; and, what was worse, it led to a painful scene, little creditable, it must be confessed, to Beethoven,

[1] The accounts given of this incident vary slightly. It was described exactly as above to Sir George Grove by the lady herself—Mme. Sabatier Ungher—during her visit to London in 1869, and the anecdote will be found in Grove's *Analytical Essays on Beethoven's Nine Symphonies*—a book which every lover of Beethoven's music should endeavour to possess.

although the effect of all these worries and disappointments upon a naturally irritable and sensitive brain suggests a plea in mitigation of his conduct which few will be disinclined to admit. He invited Schindler, Schuppanzigh, and Umlaut to dinner, and before the festivities commenced, suddenly burst into a volley of abuse, and accused them all in round terms of conspiring to defraud him. Needless to add, the party broke up in confusion; the guests lost a dinner, and their host—for a time, at any rate—three of his trustiest comrades.

In his new-born anxiety to make and save money for the benefit of his nephew, Beethoven now negotiated personally with courts, patrons, and publishers for the sale of various works. An advantageous offer, made at this time by the Philharmonic Society, would have enriched him by £800 had he consented to pay a visit to London; but after the fracas with his three friends this project fell through; and meanwhile the Mass was subscribed for but slowly. In his desire to recover lost ground, Beethoven supplemented the labours of composition with others of a more prosaic kind, for which he was proverbially unfitted. Abortive schemes for bringing out "collected editions" of his works, sales at unfavourable prices, and innumerable misunderstandings and complications speedily followed this ill-judged excursion into the domain of business. After offering the Mass and the Symphony in various quarters, he sold them to Schott, the publisher of Mayence, with whom he had just established relations. But in spite of all other occupations, composition was still continued with vigour. "Apollo and the Muses will not deliver me over to the hand of death. There are yet many things the spirit inspires me with, that I must finish. I feel as if I had written scarcely a note."

The religious element in Beethoven's character, traces of which are so frequently seen in his letters, strengthened and deepened as age and troubles increased. A noble ideal of duty and of self-denial was constantly before him, and how profound was his sense of responsibility to the art he loved, as well as to his fellow-men, we have the record of his life-work to prove. Theological talk, however, was little to his taste; and of external religious observances we hear almost nothing. *Laborare est orare* seems to have been his motto through life. A line of a hymn, *Gott allein ist unser Herr*, found by Mr. Nottebohm, scribbled in the sketch-book of the year 1818, furnishes one evidence, among many others, of the devotional spirit which pervaded Beethoven's character. A few years before his death he copied out, and kept constantly before him on his writing-table, the following sentences, said to be taken from the Temple of Isis:—

"I am that which is;

"I am all that is, that was, and that shall be. No mortal man has lifted my veil.

"He proceeds from Himself alone, and to Him alone do all things owe their existence."

Nominally—but only nominally—Beethoven was a Roman Catholic, and he received the last sacraments of the Church on his death-bed.

We may pause a moment before a picture—furnished by one who often frequented his favourite tavern—of the composer in those later days when his deafness had become confirmed beyond all hope of recovery; a picture full of pathos and sad premonition of the last scene of all.

"A sturdy-looking man of middle height, gray hair like a mane flowing from his lion-like head; with a wandering look in his gray eyes; unsteady in his movements as one moving in a dream."

Every one showed him the greatest respect whenever he entered the room. He would sit apart at a table with a glass of beer and a long pipe, and close his eyes.

If a friend spoke—or rather bawled to him—he would look up, draw a pocket-book and pencil from his breast, and in the shrill voice peculiar to deaf people, bid his visitor write down what he had to say. "He replied sometimes verbally, sometimes in writing; but always readily and kindly."

Schubert—the young strong-winged genius whose career of song has just begun—is present on one of those evenings. When the old man takes from his simple gray overcoat another and larger note-book, and traces something with half-closed eyes, a companion asks: "What is he writing?"—"He is composing."—"But he writes words, not notes?"—"That is his way; he usually indicates the course of his ideas for a piece of music by words, with a few notes here and there"—not a very accurate account, by the way, of Beethoven's usual method. And thus—alone in the midst of company—he pursues his work, and the younger men, sinking their voices to a needless whisper, glance from time to time pitifully and reverentially in the direction of the great cloud-compeller.

The last symphony and the last pianoforte sonatas had been written—for the projected tenth symphony, like the *Requiem*, the opera for Naples, and the overture on B-A-C-H, was destined never to be accomplished—and now Beethoven was at work upon three Quartets, written in a language as far ahead of his time as was the Ninth Symphony. They were composed at the instigation of Prince Galitzin, a Russian nobleman, who opened the subject by correspondence in 1824. The fame of the friend of Count Browne, of the composer of the *Rasoumoffsky Quartets*, and works dedicated to the Emperor and Empress of Russia, had long since extended to St. Petersburg, so that the remuneration offered by the prince was sufficiently handsome; but though the Quartets were written, the promised money was never paid. The circumstance has been variously accounted for, and if all the facts were known, it is possible that reasons might be found for modifying the harsh construction generally placed upon Galitzin's conduct. For Beethoven's way of dealing with his compositions at this time was, to say the least, singular, the object uppermost in his mind being, apparently, to turn them into ready money as quickly as possible. Schott bought the first of the Quartets—that in E♭—for fifty ducats in advance, at about the same time he bought the overture *Weihe des Hauses*, the *Opferlied*, for solo, chorus, and orchestra, *In Allen guten*

Stunden, a setting for solo, chorus, and wind instruments, of Goethe's words, and sundry smaller pieces. For the first performance of the Quartet in E♭, the services were engaged of the doughty four, Schuppanzigh, Weiss, Linke, and Holtz—the latter, a clever young violinist and violoncellist, of convivial tastes, who obtained considerable ascendancy over Beethoven in these days. That neither anxiety nor growing infirmity had been sufficient to crush the composer's sense of humour, is clear from a whimsical note, to which he exacted each executant's signature, by way of reminder of former triumphs, and of the old adage, "noblesse oblige."

"My good Friends,

"Each will herewith receive his part; but he must promise obedience, and vow to exert his utmost to distinguish himself and to emulate the zeal of his companions.

"Every one who wishes to join in the performance must sign this paper."

[The four signatures follow.]

The second Quartet (known as the third), in A minor, published in 1827 by Schlesinger, contains a noteworthy feature in the beautiful adagio, *in modo lidico*, entitled, *Song of Thanksgiving offered to the Deity by a Convalescent*, written to commemorate the composer's recovery from a severe illness that occurred during the winter of 1824, just as he had completed the first of the series.

In the month of October 1826, painful events connected with that never-ending source of misery, his nephew Carl, induced Beethoven to take up his abode in quarters which, for several reasons, were distasteful to him—the country house of his brother Johann at Gneixendorf, near Krems, on the Danube.

The former apothecary of Linz had turned his commercial instincts to profitable account, and acquired a fortune, or the basis of a fortune, by undertaking army contracts during the war-time of 1809. Pompous, vulgar-minded, and niggardly, and married to a woman whom Beethoven for long had refused to acknowledge as a sister-in-law, Johann was utterly insensible to the honour conferred upon him by the presence of such a guest. It may be questioned, indeed, whether the "land proprietor" did not consider the honour to be on the other side.

As for Carl, the story of his youth was a commonplace story of continuous mishap, failure, and disgrace, brought about by bad counsel and selfish indulgence; and these evils were aggravated by the unsettled life he had led. During the lawsuit, he was passed backwards and forwards from one guardian to another, the mother meanwhile losing no opportunity of poisoning his mind against his long-suffering relative. Many careers were tried, but he succeeded in none. He was expelled from the University after attending a philosophical course, and duly forgiven. Commerce was then suggested, and with this view he was placed in the school of the Polytechnic Institute, of which Herr Reisser, joint guardian with Beethoven over Carl, was the vice-president. The letters addressed to the youth by his uncle during this period—there were no fewer than twenty-nine in the summer of 1825—full of solicitude and kindly counsel, are painful reading. But the inevitable end came. Carl submitted himself to an examination without sufficient preparatory study, failed, and in his despair attempted suicide; in consequence of which escapade, he was ordered by the police to quit Vienna within twenty-four hours.

Self-denying and beautiful as was Beethoven's conduct towards this wrong-headed nephew, it is very likely that his habitual roughness of manner when irritated caused his admonitions to take at times a form particularly unpalatable to the young man. "It's done now. Torment me no more with reproofs and complaints," wrote Carl; and on one occasion the singular remark escaped him—"I have grown worse, because my uncle wanted me to be better."

Thus quarrels, reconciliations, reproaches, and promises followed one upon the other; and throughout, with all a father's care and devotion, Beethoven continued working and saving for the benefit of the youth upon whom his affections were now centred. At length, thanks to the interposition of Stephan Breuning, a cadetship was obtained for him in the regiment of Baron von Stutterheim, in gratitude to whom the composer dedicated the String Quartet completed in that year, Op. 131, in C sharp minor.

In October 1826, while arrangements connected with the appointment were still pending, both uncle and nephew took refuge in the house at Gneixendorf. One of Beethoven's motives for undertaking this visit was a hope that his brother might be induced to make his will in favour of the family ne'er-do-well—a question that had already caused some bickering between the two uncles. Dreary and inhospitable as were his surroundings, Beethoven was probably too much engrossed in his music, and too long accustomed to the isolation caused by his deafness, to be greatly troubled by them.

For an onlooker the situation was one that could hardly fail to inspire a feeling of deep sadness. Glad enough of an opportunity to display his own importance, Johann took his brother with him on his rounds; but was little concerned, apparently, to introduce him to his friends. Even in that out-of-the-way district, however, there was a magic in the name of Beethoven. Many of the good people thereabouts, when they discovered the identity of the careworn, reserved old man who accompanied the "land proprietor," eyed him with silent reverence. At one house the hostess glanced towards the bench, on which a stranger sat apart from the rest, modestly and mournfully, whilst Johann talked with her. She thought he was a servant, and good-naturedly handed him wine in an earthenware jug. Later, when her husband returned, he told her who that stranger was. It was Beethoven. Another day the brothers went to talk over business with the clerk of the Syndic, Sterz, at Langenlois. "Who, think you, was that old man who came just now with the Squire?" The clerk did not know—thought he was "an imbecile." It was Beethoven. Toilers in the chill autumn fields stopped to follow with their eyes the lonely musician, as he wandered about waving his hands and singing. Sometimes he would slacken his pace, and, coming to a standstill, jot down something in the inevitable note-book

—for the music went on, in spite of all troubles and discomforts, and it was here that he completed the String Quartet in F, and the new finale to the B♭ sonata.

Michael Kren, the servant deputed by the mistress of the household to wait upon their guest, has described the way in which Beethoven usually passed a day at Gneixendorf. He occupied a parlour and bedroom at the corner of the house commanding a view of the garden and courtyard. The economical sister-in-law refused him a fire. At half-past four in the morning Michael would find him at his table writing, beating time with his hands and feet, and singing and humming. Breakfast was served to the family at half-past seven, after which he would immediately hurry out of the house into the fields. The dinner hour was half-past twelve; and this over he would retire to his fireless room until about three o'clock, and then once again sally forth; but he was never out of doors after sunset. After supper, which took place at half-past seven, he returned to his room to work till ten, and then retired to bed.

As time went on the discomfort increased. The parsimonious Johann informed his brother he would be charged for board and lodging; Johann's wife by no means improved on acquaintance; and Carl, under her influence, grew ever more insulting and unmanageable. On a cold day, in an open chaise—for no close carriage was to be had—Beethoven, accompanied by his nephew, took his departure. The visit, unpropitious from the beginning, had a tragic end. During the drive the composer caught a severe cold which attacked the stomach, and, arrived at his lodgings, which were now in the Schwarzspanierhaus, took to his bed. The result of that fatal journey was a severe attack of inflammation of the lungs and dropsy.

Two eminent doctors, Staudenheim and Braunhofer, who attended him during his former illness, had been dismissed in the unceremonious manner so frequently shown by Beethoven towards his medical advisers, and when sent for, at first refused their services. The assistance so urgently needed in Beethoven's case was further delayed by his nephew's neglect; for once back in Vienna, that worthy made haste to return to his old haunts, and, leaving his uncle to the care of servants, sought consolation at the billiard-table. Thus two days were allowed to pass before a doctor was summoned. Through the good offices of a billiard-marker, one at last was found in Dr. Wawruch, a man far inferior in ability to those who had attended Beethoven on the former occasion, and quite unfit, according to Breuning, to be intrusted with so important a life. Malfatti, to whom also the composer had given serious offence some years before, was now applied to. At first he refused; but after considerable difficulty was persuaded to bury old grievances, on the understanding that he should act jointly with Wawruch. As soon as Malfatti entered upon the scene a total change of treatment was adopted; and for the enervating herb decoctions, iced punch was now substituted. With his wonted shrewd perception of a doctor's weak points, the patient quickly detected Wawruch's incompetence, and expressed his sense of it in the usual uncompromising manner, turning to the wall and exclaiming, "Ach der Esel!" whenever that person entered the room.

In Malfatti, on the other hand, Beethoven showed the greatest confidence; and the temporary relief that followed upon the new treatment rendered him again hopeful and eager for work. This, however, was forbidden. As the dropsical symptoms became more serious, the operation of tapping was resorted to, and even during this process Beethoven's grim sense of humour did not desert him. The surgeon who operated, caused him to think of Moses striking the rock; and when the water flowed he exclaimed, "Better water from the stomach than from the pen!"

Among the first to hasten to the composer's bedside were his old friend Schindler—full ready to forget old scores—and Stephan Breuning; the latter accompanied by his son Gerhard, a boy of eleven, who greatly contributed to the sick man's comfort by many a little service. Brother Johann, Tobias and Carl Haslinger, Diabelli, Holtz, and some four or five others also came, and in March Hummel, accompanied by his young pupil Ferdinand Hiller, sought and obtained an interview. The list of visitors seems a strangely meagre one. Even when allowance is made for the possible absence from town of many society friends who courted and worshipped the great musician in his palmy days, and for the circumstance that for some time the fatal nature of this illness was not generally realized, the sad fact still remains, that when Beethoven lay, poor and dying, in Vienna, all his former aristocratic friends, except

Breuning, seem for the moment to have forgotten his existence; that his brother musicians for the most part were conspicuous by their absence; that even his old pupil, the Archduke Rudolph, made no sign, no inquiries, as far as we know, and no attempt to supply his necessities.

This privilege was reserved for the English Philharmonic Society, to which body belongs the credit of having come to the assistance of Beethoven at a time when he was so strangely neglected by his countrymen. The remittance promised by Prince Galitzin was never received; the proceeds of recent works had been devoted to an investment set aside rigidly for his nephew; and the later concerts, as we know, had been pecuniarily unsuccessful. At this juncture Beethoven's thoughts turned to that English Society whose good-will he had always so dearly prized. In February 1827 he wrote to Moscheles and Sir George Smart, describing his plight, and begging them to hasten on a benefit concert that had been promised him in London. After Beethoven's death the discovery of seven bank shares, of one thousand florins each, came as a surprise to many who had witnessed these straits and who were aware of the appeal to the Philharmonic Society. But Beethoven, it should be remembered, had always regarded the property in question as held in trust for Carl, so that not even the most desperate monetary pressure would have induced him to touch it. The privation, therefore, referred to by him in his letters to London was very real. The Philharmonic promptly responded by sending through Moscheles £100 on account of the impending concert, with the promise of more should it be needed. Beethoven's joyful emotion, when he received Moscheles's letter, is described by one as "heart-breaking," and the excitement of that moment, causing his wound to break out afresh, no doubt hastened the final catastrophe.

Debarred from composition by order of his medical attendants, Beethoven turned to reading, and commenced with a translation of Sir Walter Scott's *Kenilworth;* but before he had gone far in the book he flung it down impatiently, with the exclamation, "The man writes only for money." More satisfaction awaited him in the examination of some of Schubert's songs, which were then brought under his notice for the first time. "Assuredly Schubert has in him the divine fire," was his verdict. During the earlier stages of his illness his imagination was full of schemes for future work—the tenth symphony, the *Faust* music, and other great projects, which were fated to be cut short by death. Besides dictating numerous letters to friends, he occupied himself with the dedications of the Quartets in C sharp minor and F, and with the arrangement of his worldly affairs; and he derived special pleasure from a complete edition of Handel's works sent to him by Strumpff. About a year before Beethoven had written to Dr. Bach, his confidential lawyer, committing Carl to his care, and declaring the youth to be his sole heir. One of his last acts, indeed, was to add a codicil to his will to this effect; though, in deference to the urgent representations of Breuning and other friends, the capital was placed beyond his nephew's control. Soon it became evident to himself and to those about him that the time for work had passed away for ever. *Plaudite amici comœdia finita est,* he said to his old friends Breuning and Schindler.

Among the latest callers was Schubert, who, however, arrived too late to hold converse with the sufferer; and Dr. Wawruch said, "He is rapidly dying." On the morning of the 24th March, Schindler found Beethoven much changed, and so weak that it cost him an effort to utter even one or two words. It was he who first suggested to the dying master that he should receive the last sacraments of the Roman Church. To this Beethoven calmly and composedly assented. According to Frau Johann van Beethoven, after the rites had been administered, he said, "Reverend Sir, I thank you. You have brought me consolation." Schott, the publisher, had sent him a present of wine, but it came too late.

For our knowledge of what occurred on the last day of all we are dependent upon an account given by Anselm Hüttenbrenner, the composer, and the friend of Schubert. Immediately on hearing of the master's serious illness, Hüttenbrenner hurried from his native place, Gratz, and at about three o'clock in the afternoon of March 26th, 1827, entered the sick-room. He found there, besides Frau Johann, Breuning and his son, Schindler, and Joseph Tellschter, the portrait painter, all of whom, except Johann Beethoven's wife, presently left; Stephan Breuning and Schindler going together to the Währing Cemetery[1] to select a grave.

[1] The remains of Beethoven have been twice disturbed. In consequence of the neglected condition of the grave, they were exhumed and re-buried on October 13, 1863; and on June 21,

Outside the ground gleamed white with snow; and from three till past five o'clock the master lay unconscious. Suddenly the room was lit up by a vivid flash of lightning, followed by a clap of thunder. "At the sound," says the narrator, "Beethoven opened his eyes, raised his right hand, and gazed fixedly upwards for some seconds, with clenched fist and a solemn, threatening expression. . . . His hand dropped and his eyes were half-closed. My right hand supported his head; my left lay on his breast. Not another breath! not another heart-beat! The spirit of the great master had passed from this false world to the kingdom of truth. I closed his half-shut eyes and kissed his brow, mouth, hand, and eyes. At my request Frau van Beethoven cut a lock of his hair, and gave it me as a sacred memento of Beethoven's dying hour."

On the day of the funeral, the 29th March, 1827, the streets of Vienna presented an unwonted appearance. No sooner were the words passed from mouth to mouth, "Beethoven is dead!" than the Viennese, strangely apathetic until now, suddenly awoke to the magnitude of their loss. Universal sorrow prevailed, and all classes of society, from the highest to the lowest, flocked out of doors, to honour the memory of their greatest musician. The morning was fine, and towards three o'clock—the time fixed for the ceremony—the crowd

---

1888, they were removed altogether from the Währing Cemetery under circumstances which to many seemed very like desecration, and transferred to the central cemetery of Vienna at Simmering, where they now lie close to the graves of Mozart and Schubert.

increased, it is estimated, to the number of twenty thousand. "So great," says Schindler, "was the pressure round the house that it was found necessary to close the courtyard gates, within which, under an awning, stood the coffin raised upon a bier and surrounded by the mourners."

As the procession, accompanied by fifteen friends of the deceased holding torches, was carried from the Schwarzspannierhaus to the church of the Minorites, the throng became so dense that the help of soldiers was required to clear the way. The bearers were eight members of the opera, and Breuning, Johann van Beethoven, and Mosel were the chief mourners. During the service a melody by the composer, arranged for the occasion as a *miserere*, was sung by a male choir and played by four trombones. Afterwards, at the cemetery gates, Anschütz, the actor, recited a funeral oration written by Grillparzer. Three laurel wreaths were placed upon the coffin by Hummel before it was lowered.

Among the vast crowd assembled at the funeral, many who had known Beethoven by sight only, returned home with saddened hearts. Never again were they to see the figure once so familiar to their streets. The voice that had grown prophetic in those latter days was now silent for ever.

[1] CATALOGUE

OF

BEETHOVEN'S PRINTED WORKS.

Abbreviations: PF. = Pianoforte. V. = Violin. Va. = Viola. C. = 'cello. C. bass = Contrabass. Clav. = Clavecin. Clar. = Clarinet. Ob. = Oboe. Fl. = Flute. Orch. = Orchestra. Aut. = Autograph. ann. = announced. arrt. = arrangement.

I. WORKS WITH OPUS NUMBERS.

Op.	*Description.*	*Composed.*	*Dedicated to*
1	Three Trios, PF. V. C. (in E♭, G, C minor).	Before April 1795.	Prince Carl von Lichnowsky.
2	Three Sonatas, Clav. or PF. (F minor, A, and C).	... ...	Joseph Haydn.
3	Grand Trio, V. Va. C. (E♭).	1792, at Bonn.	
4	Grand Quintet, V. V. Va. Va. C. (E♭).		
5	Two Grand Sonatas. PF. C. (F, G minor).	... ...	Frederick William II. of Prussia.
6	Sonata, 4 hands, Clav. or PF. (D).		
7	Grand Sonata, Clav. or PF. (E♭).	... ...	Countess Babette von Keglevics.
8	Serenade, V. Va. C. (D)		
9	Three Trios, V. Va. C. (G, D, C minor).	... ...	Count v. Browne.
10	Three Sonatas, Clav. or PF. (C minor, F, D).	Before July 7, 1798.	Countess Browne.
11	Grand Trio, PF. Clav. (or V.) C. (B♭).	... ...	Countess v. Thun.
12	Three Sonatas, Clav. or PF. V.	... ...	A. Salieri.
13	Grand Sonata Pathétique, Clav. or PF. (C minor).	... ...	Prince Carl von Lichnowsky.
14	Two Sonatas, PF. (E, G).	... ...	Baroness v. Braun.
15	Grand Concerto, PF. and Orch. (C). (Really the second.)	At latest 1796.	Princess Odeschalchi, *née* Keglevics.
16	Grand Quintet, PF. Ob. Clar. Bassoon, Horn or V. Va. C. (E♭). Arrd. by Beethoven as a quartet for PF. V. Va. C. Also arrd. as string quartet and marked Op. 75.	... ...	

[1] The materials for this list have been extracted, by kind permission, from the Appendix to Vol. IV. of Sir George Grove's *Dictionary of Music and Musicians*, to which readers may be referred for further interesting details.

Op.	*Description.*	*Composed.*	*Dedicated to*
17	Sonata, PF. Horn or C. (F).	Before April 18, 1801.	Baroness v. Braun.
18	Six Quartets, V. V. Va. C. (F, G, D, C minor, A, B♭).	No. 1 and 6 in 1800.	Prince von Lobkowitz.
19	Concerto PF. and Orch. (B♭). (Really the first.) See No. 151.	Before March 1795.	Charles Nikl Noble de Niklsberg.
20	Septet, V. Va. Horn, Clar. Bassoon, C. C bass. (E♭).	Before April 2, 1800.	Empress Maria Theresa.
21	Grand Symphony (C). The first.	Before Apr. 2, 1800.	Baron v. Swieten.
22	Grand Sonata, PF. (B♭).	Before end of 1800.	Count v. Browne.
23	Two Sonatas, PF. V. (A minor, F).	First two movements of Sonata 1, composed in 1800.	Count M. von Fries.
24	Sonata in F, PF. V. (Op. 23), Op. 24, was originally PF. score of Prometheus, now Op. 43.	... ...	*idem.*
25	Serenade, Fl. V. Va. (see Op. 41).		
26	Grand Sonata, Clav. or PF. (A♭).	... ...	Prince C. Lichnowsky.
27	No. 1 Sonata quasi una Fantasia, Clav. or PF. (E♭).	... ...	Princess J. Liechtenstein.
	No. 2 Sonata quasi una Fantasia, Clav. or PF. (C♯ minor), ('Moonlight').	... ...	Countesa Giulietta Guicciardi.
28	Grand Sonata, PF. (D), ('Pastoral').	1801.	Joseph Edlen von Sonnenfels.
29	Quintet, V.V. Va. Va. C. (C).	1801.	Count M. v. Fries.
30	Three Sonatas, PF. V. (A, C minor, G).	1802.	Alexander I. Emperor of Russia.
31	Three Sonatas, Clav. or PF. (G, D minor, E♭).	Nos. 1 and 2, 1802.	
32	Song, 'An die Hoffnung,' Tiedge's 'Urania' (E♭).		
33	Seven Bagatelles, PF. (E♭. C, F, A, C, D, F minor).	1782—1802.	
34	Six Variations on an original theme, PF. (F).	Close of 1802.	Princess Odeschalchi, *née* Keglevics.
35	[15] Variations with a fugue, on theme from Prometheus, PF. (E♭).	1802.	Count M. Lichnowsky.
36	Symphony No. 2. Orch. (D).	Close of 1802. First performance, April 5, 1803.	Prince Carl Lichnowsky.
37	Grand Concerto, PF. and Orch. (C minor).	1800.	
38	Trio, PF. Clar. V. or C. (E♭), arranged by author from Septet, Op. 20.	1802.	Prof. J. A. Schmidt, with Preface.
39	Two Preludes, through all 12 major keys, PF. or Organ.	1789.	
40	Romance, V. and Orch. (G).	1803.	
41	Serenade, PF. F. or V. (D), from the Serenade, Op. 25; revised by composer.		
42	Notturno, PF. Va. (D), arranged from the Serenade, Op. 8.		
43	The Men of Prometheus, Ballet, Nos. 1—16.		

Op.	*Description.*	*Composed.*	*Dedicated to*
44	Fourteen Variations, PF. V. C. (E♭).	1792 or 1793.	
45	Three Grand Marches, PF. 4 hands (C, E♭, D).	... ...	Princess Esterhazy, *née* Liechtenstein.
46	Adelaide, by Matthisson, Cantata, for Soprano with PF. (B♭).	1795 (?).	Matthisson.
47	Sonata ['Kreutzer'], PF. V. (A).	Mar. 17, 1803.	R. Kreutzer.
48	Six Songs by Gellert, for Soprano:—Bitten; Die Liebe des Nächsten; Vom Tode; Die Ehre Gottes; Gottes Macht; Busslied.	... ...	Count Browne.
49	Two Easy Sonatas, PF. (G minor, G major).	Not later than 1802.	
50	Romance, V. and Orch. (F).		
51	Two Rondos, PF. (C, G).	... ...	Countess Henrietta v. Lichnowsky.
52	Eight songs:—Urian's Reise (Claudius); Feuerfarb (Mereau); Das Liedchen v. d. Ruhe (Ueltzen); Mailied (Goethe); Molly's Abschied (Bürger); Die Liebe (Lessing); Marmotte (Goethe); Das Blümchen Wunderhold (Bürger).	Mostly very early.	
53	Grand Sonata ['Waldstein'], PF. (C). See No. 170.	1804.	Count von Waldstein.
54	['LIst] Sonata, PF. (F).		
55	Sinfonia eroica, No. 3 (E♭).	Aug. 1804.	Prince von Lobkowitz.
56	Grand Concerto [Triple], PF. V. C. and Orch. (C).	1804.	Prince von Lobkowitz.
57	['LIVth'] Sonata, PF. (F minor), so-called 'Appassionata.'	1804.	Count Francis von Brunswick.
58	Fourth Concerto, PF. and Orch. (G).	1805.	Archduke Rudolph of Austria.
59	Three Quartets ['Rasoumoffsky'], V.V. Va. C. (F, E minor, C). (7th, 8th, and 9th.)	Before Feb. 1807.	Count von Rasoumoffsky.
60	Fourth Symphony (B♭).	1806.	Count Oppersdorf.
61	Concerto, V. and Orch. (D).	1806. First played Dec. 23, 1806.	Stephan v. Breuning.
	Concerto, PF. and Orch., arranged by author from his First Concerto for Violin (D).	April 1807.	Madame v. Breuning.
62	Overture to Coriolan.	April 1807.	M. [H. J.] de Collin.
63	Scena ed Aria, 'Ah, perfido!' Sopr. and Orch.	Prague, 1796.	Countess v. Clary.
64	Twelve Variations on 'Ein Mädchen' (Zauberflöte), PF. C. (F).		
67	Symphony, No. 5 (C minor).	Begun 1805; first played Dec. 22, 1808.	Prince von Lobkowitz and Count Rasoumoffsky.
68	Pastoral Symphony, No. 6 (F).	Kattendyke, Arnheim.	Prince Lobkowitz and Count Rasoumoffsky.
69	Grand Sonata, PF. C. (A).	... ...	'My friend Baron von Gleichenstein.'

Op.	*Description.*	*Composed.*	*Dedicated to*
70	Two Trios, PF. V. C. (D, E♭).	Close of 1808.	Countess Marie v. Erdödy.
71	Saxtet, Clar. Clar. Cor. Cor. Fag. Fag. (E♭).	Early.	
72	Fidelio, or Wedded Love.	Begun 1803. Produced in 3 Acts, Nov. 20, 1805; Overture 'No. 2.' Reduced to 2 Acts and reproduced Mar. 29, 1806; Overture 'No. 3.' Much revised and again produced May 23, 1814. Overture in E first played at second performance. Overture 'No. 1,' composed for a proposed performance in Prague, 1807, but not played. See Op. 138.	Archduke Rudolph.
73	Concerto, PF. and Orch. (E♭), the Fifth.	1809.	Archduke Rudolph.
74	Quartet ['Harfen'], V. V. Va. C. (E♭). (The 10th.)	1809.	Prince Lobkowitz.
75	Six Songs, Sopr. and PF. 'Kennst du das Land,' 'Herz mein Herz,' and 'Es war einmal,' Goethe; 'Mit Liebesblick,' Halem; 'Einst wohnten' and 'Zwar schuf das Glück,' Reissig. Op. 75 is also marked to an arrt. of Op. 16 as a string quartet.	No. 1, May 1810. No. 4, 1803.	Princess von Kinsky.
76	[6] Variations, PF. (D). See Op. 113.	1809 (?).	'To his friend Oliva.'
77	Fantaisie, PF. (G minor).	1808 (?).	Count Francis von Brunswick.
78	Sonata, PF. (F♯).	Oct. 1809.	Countess Therèse von Brunswick.
79	Sonatina, PF. (G).	Before Dec. 1808.	
80	Fantasia, PF. Orch. Chorus. Words by Kuffner. The theme of the variations is Beethoven's song 'Gegenliebe.' See No. 254.	Performed Dec. 22, 1808.	Maxmilian Joseph, King of Bavaria.
81*a*	Sonata, PF. (E♭), 'Les Adieux, l'Absence, et le Retour.'	May 4, 1809.	Archduke Rudolph.
81*b*	Sextet, V. V. Va. C. 2 Cors. (E♭).		
82	Four Ariettas and a duet, Sopr. and PF. Words by Metastasio. 1. 'Dimmi ben mio.' 2. 'T'intendo, si.' 3. 'Che fa, il mio bene' (*buffa*). 4. 'Che fa il mio bene' (*seria*). 5. 'Odi l'aura.' German words by Schreiber	No. 4, 1809.—*Aut.* No. 1, Artaria.	

Op.	*Description.*	*Composed*	*Dedicated to*
83	Three Songs by Goethe, Sopr. and PF. 1. 'Trocknet nicht.' 2. 'Was zieht mir.' 3. 'Kleine Blumen.'	1810.	Princess von Kinsky.
84	Music to Goethe's Egmont. Overture. 1. Song, 'Die Trommel.' 2. Entracte I. 3. Entracte II. 4. Song, 'Freudvoll und leidvoll.' 5. Entracte III. 6. Entracte IV. 7. Clara's death. 8. Melodrama. 9. Battle Symphony.	1810.—*Aut.* of Overture, F. Hauser, Munich. Do. of No. 8, Frl. Kistner, Leipzig. First performance, May 24, 1810.	
85	Christus am Oelberge. 'Mount of Olives,' S. T. B. Chorus, Orch.	1800. First performance April 5, 1803, Vienna.	
86	Mass, S. A. T. B. Chorus, Orch. (C).	1807. First performance, Sep. 8, 1807, Eisenstadt.	Pr. Nicholas Esterhazy de Galantha.
87	Grand Trio for V. V. Va. (C) taken, with Beethoven's approbation, from a MS. Trio for 2 Oboes and Engl. horn.	1794 (?).—*Aut.* of original, Artaria.	
88	Song, 'Das Glück der Freundschaft,' S. and PF. (A).		
89	Polonaise, PF. (C).	1814 (?).	Empress of Russia.
90	Sonata, PF. (E minor).	Aug. 16, 1814.	Count Moritz von Lichnowsky.
91	Wellington's Victory, or the Battle of Vittoria, Orch. Battle fought June 21, 1813. News reached Vienna, July 27, 1813.	First performance, Dec. 8, 1813.	Prince Regent of England.
92	Seventh Grand Symphony, Orch. (A).	May 13, 1812.—First performance Dec. 8, 1813.	Count von Fries. Empress of Russia.
93	Eighth Grand Symphony, Orch. (F).	Linz, Oct. 1812.—First performance, Feb. 27, 1814.	
94	Song, 'An die Hoffnung,' by Tiedge, S. and PF.	1816 (?).	Princess Kinsky.
95	Quartet, V. V. Va. C. (F minor). (The 11th.)	Oct. 1810.	'His friend N. Zmeskall von Domanovetz.'
96	Sonata, PF. V. (G).	1812. First performance Jan. 1813, by Archduke Rudolph and Rode.	
97	Trio, PF. V. C. (B♭).	1811. Mar. 3—26.	
98	Six Songs, 'An die ferne (*aut.* entfernte) Geliebte, Liederkreis,' by A. Jeitteles.	April 1816.	Prince Joseph von Lobkowitz.
99	Song, 'Der Mann von Wort,' by Kleinschmid (G).		
100	Duet, 'Merkenstein near Baden,' by J. B. Rupprecht (E).	Dec. 22, 1814 (?).	Count v. Dietrichstein (Dedn. by Rupprecht).
101	Sonata, PF. (Hammer-klavier) (A).	First performance Feb. 18, 1816.	Baroness Dorothea Ertmann.

Op.	*Description.*	*Composed.*	*Dedicated to*
102	Two Sonatas, PF. C. (C, D).	July and August 1815.	No dedication. Countess Erdödy.
103	Octet, 2 Ob. 2 Clars. 2 Cors. 2 Fag. (E♭). The original of Op. 4.		
104	Quintet, V. V. Va. Va C. (C minor), arranged by Beethoven from Op. 1, no. 3.	Aug. 14, 1817.	
105	Six very easy themes varied, PF. F. or V.	1818, 1819.	
106	Grand Sonata, PF. (Hammer-klavier) (B♭).	1818.	Archduke Rudolph.
107	Ten [national] themes with variations, PF. F. or V.	1818–20.	
108	Twenty-five Scotch Songs, 2 Voices and small chorus, PF. V. C.	May 1815 (?).	Pr. Radzivil.
109	Sonata, PF. (E).	1820 (?).	Frl. Maximiliana Brentano.
110	Sonata, PF. (Hammer-klavier), (A♭).	Dec. 25, 1821.	
111	Sonata, PF. (C minor); the last sonata.	Jan. 13, 1822.	Archduke Rudolph (ded. by publishers).
112	Calm sea and prosperous voyage. S. A T. B. and Orch. Goethe's words.	1815.	Goethe.
113	The Ruins of Athens. Kotzebue's words. Chorus and Orch.	1811. Produced Feb. 9, 1812.	King of Prussia.
114	March and Chorus (E♭) from 'Ruins of Athens,' for the Dedication of the Josephstadt Theatre, Vienna.		
115	Grand Overture in C, sometimes called 'Namensfeier.'	'Am ersten Weinmonat (October) 1814.' Produced Dec. 25, 1815.	Prince Radzivil.
116	Terzetto, 'Tremate,' S. T. B. (B♭).	1802.	
117	King Stephen, Grand Overture (E♭) and 9 numbers.	1811, for performance with Op. 113 on Feb. 9, 1812.	
118	Elegiac Song, S. A. T. B. and Strings (E). In memory of Eleonora Pasqualati, died Aug. 23, 1811.	'Summer 1814.'	'His friend' Baron Pasqualati.
119	New Bagatelles, easy and agreeable, PF. (G minor, C, D, A, C minor, G, G, C, C, A minor, A, B♭, G).	Nov. 1–6, 1822.	
120	33 Variations on a Waltz (by Diabelli) (C).	1823 (?).	Mad. Antonia von Brentano.
121*a*	Adagio, Variations, and Rondo, PF. V. C. (G).		
121*b*	Opferlied, by Matthisson, Sopr. with Chorus and Orch.	1822 (?). The original version 1802. Produced April 4, 1824.	
122	Bundeslied, by Goethe (B♭), S. A. Chorus and Wind.	1823.	
123	Mass in D, 'Messe Solennelle.'	1823.	Archduke Rudolph.
124	Overture in C, called 'Weihe des Hauses.' Written for opening of Josephstadt Theatre, Vienna.	End Sept. 1822.	Prince N. Galitzin.

Op.	*Description.*	*Composed.*	*Dedicated to*
125	Symphony No. 9 (D minor), Grand Orch. S. A. T. B. and Chorus.	1823.	King of Prussia.
126	Six Bagatelles, PF. (G, G minor, E, B minor, G, E♭, E♭).	Early in 1823.	
127	Quartet, V.V. Va. C. (The 12th) (E♭).	1824.	Prince N. Galitzin.
128	Arietta, 'The Kiss,' by Weisse.	End of 1822.	
129	Rondo a capriccio, PF. (G), 'Fury over a lost groschen, vented in a caprice.'		
130	Quartet, VV. Va. C. (B♭). (The 13th.)	1825 and (finale) Nov. 1826.—*Aut.* First movement Mendelssohns, Berlin; second do. F. Gross; third do. J. Hellmesberger: Cavatina, Artaria; Finale Ascher—all in Vienna. Produced with Op. 133 as finale, Mar. 21, 1826.	Prince N. Galitzin.
131	Quartet, V.V. Va. C. (C♯ minor). 'Fourth Quartet.' (The 14th.)	Oct. 1826.—*Aut.* First movement, Mendelssohns, Berlin. *Revised MS.* Schotts, Mainz.	Baron von Stutterheim.
132	Quartet, V.V. Va. C. (A minor), 'Second Quartet.' (The 15th.)	1825: Produced Nov. 6, 1825.—*Aut.* Mendelssohns, Berlin.	Prince N. Galitzin.
133	Grand Fugue, V.V. Va. C. (B♭) 'Tantôt libre, tantôt recherchée.' Originally the Finale to Op. 130.	*Aut.* ('Ouvertura'), Artaria, Vienna.	Archduke Rudolph.
134	Grand Fugue (Op. 133), arranged by the Author for PF. 4 hands.	... ...	Archduke Rudolph.
135	Quartet, V.V. Va. C. (F)—(the last).	Gneixendorf. Oct. 30, 1826.—*Aut.* of second and fourth movements formerly with Ascher, Vienna. *Aut.* of the parts, Schlesinger, Baden-Baden.	'His friend Johann Wolfmayer.'
136	Der glorreiche Augenblick ('the glorious moment'), Cantata, S.A.T.B. Chorus and Orch.; words by A. Weissenbach. 6 numbers. Also as Preis der Tonkunst ('Praise of Music') by F. Rochlitz.	Sept. 1814. Produced Nov. 29, 1814.—*Aut.* C. Haslinger, Vienna.	The Sovereigns of Austria, Russia, and Prussia.
137	Fugue, V.V. Va. C. (D). Composed for a collection of B.'s works pro-	Nov. 28, 1817.	

Op.	Description.	Composed.	Dedicated to
	jected by Haslinger, now in the Gesellschaft der Musikfreunde, Vienna.		
138	Overture, Orch. (C), known as 'Leonora, no. 1,' but really Leonora, no. 3. See Op. 72.	1807 (?). *Revised MS. score.* C. Haslinger, Vienna.	

II. WORKS WITHOUT OPUS NUMBERS.

1. FOR ORCHESTRA, AND ORCHESTRAL INSTRUMENTS.

No.			
139	12 Minuets, D, B♭, G, E♭, C, A, D, B♭, G, E♭, C, F.	Before Nov. 22, 1795.—*Rev. MS. Parts,* Artaria, Vienna.	
140	12 Deutsche Tänze, C, A, F, B♭, E♭, G, C, A, F, D, G. C.	Before Nov. 22, 1795.	
141	12 Contretänze, C, A, D, B♭, E♭, C, E♭, C, A, C, G, E♭. N.B. No. 7 is the dance used in the Finale of Prometheus, the Eroica, etc. No. 11 also used in Finale of Prometheus.	Nos. 2, 9, 10, 1802.	
142	Minuet of congratulation (E♭), for Hensler, Director of New Josephstadt Theatre.	Nov. 1822.	
143	Triumphal March, for Kuffner's 'Tarpeia' or 'Hersilia' (C).	Before Mar. 26, 1813. *Revised* Parts, C. Haslinger, Vienna.	
144	Military March (D).	Before June 4, 1816.	
145	Military March (F), (Zapfenstreich). For the Carrousel on Aug. 25, 1810.	1809.	
146	Rondino (E♭), 2 Ob. 2 Clar. 2 Cors. 2 Fags.	Very early.—*Aut.* C. A. Spina, Vienna.	
147	3 Duos, Clar. and Fag. (C, F, B♭).		
148	Allegro con Brio, V. Orch. (C). Fragment of 1st movement of a V. Concerto. Completed by Jos. Hellmesberger.	1800? — *Aut.* Library of the Gesellschaft der Musikfreunde, Vienna.	Dr. G. von Breuning.
149	Musik zu einem Ritterballet.	1791 (?).	

2. FOR PIANOFÔRTE, WITH AND WITHOUT ACCOMPANIMENT.

150	Sonatina for the Mandoline and Cembalo (C minor).	*Aut.* British Museum Add. MSS. 29,801.	
151	Rondo, PF. and Orch. (B♭). Probably finished by Czerny. Perhaps intended for Op. 19.	*Aut.* Diabelli.	

No.	Description.	Composed.	Dedicated to
152	3 Quartets, PF. V. Va. C. (E♭, D, C). N.B. Adagio of No. 3 is employed in Op. 2, No. 1.	1785. — *Aut.* Artaria.	
153	Trio, PF. V. C. (E♭).	1785 (?).—*Aut.* Wegeler.	
154	Trio in one movement, PF. V. C. (B♭).	June 2, 1812.—*Aut.* Brentanos at Frankfort.	
155	Rondo, Allegro, PF. and V. (G).	Probably sent to Eleonora von Breuning in 1794.	
156	12 Variations on 'Si vuol ballare,' PF. and V. (F).	... ...	Eleonora von Breuning.
157	12 Variations on 'See the conquering hero,' PF. and C. (G).	... ...	Princess Lichnowsky.
158	7 Variations on 'Bei Männern,' PF. and C. (E♭).	Jan. 1, 1802.	Count von Browne.
159	Variations on a theme by Count Waldstein, PF. 4 hands (C).		
160	Air with [6] Variations on Goethe's 'Ich denke dein,' PF. 4 hands (D).	1800.	Countess Josephine Deym and Countess Theresa Brunswick.
161	3 Sonatas, PF. (E♭, F minor, D).	'These Sonatas and the Dressler Variations my first work,' L. v. B.	Elector Maximilian Frederic of Cologne.
162	Sonata [called Easy], PF. (C), two movements only, the second completed by F. Ries.	... ...	Eleonora von Breuning.
163	2 Sonatinas, PF. (G, F). Not certainly Beethoven's.		
164	Rondo, Allegretto, PF. (A).		
165	Minuet, PF. (E♭).	1783 (?).	
166	Prelude, PF. (F minor).	1785 (?).	
167	6 Minuets, PF. (C, G, E♭, B♭, D, C). Perhaps written for Orch.		
168	7 Ländler dances (all in D).		
169	6 Ländler dances (all in D but No. 4 in D minor), also for VV. and C.	1802.	
170	Andante [favori] PF. (F), said to have been intended for Op. 53.	1804 (?).	
171	6 Allemandes, PF. and V., No. 6, in G, for PF.		
172	Ziemlich lebhaft, PF. (C minor).	Aug. 14, 1818, written by request.	
173	Bagatelle, PF. (A minor).		
174	Andante maestoso (C), arranged from the sketch for a Quintet and called 'Beethovens letzter musikalische Gedanke.'	Nov. 1826 (?).	
175	10 Cadences to Beethoven's PF. Concertos in C, B♭, C minor, G and D (arrt. of Violin Concerto, see Op. 61). Also 2 to Mozart's PF. Concerto in D minor.		

No.	Description.	Composed.	Dedicated to
176	[9] Variations and a March by Dressler, Harpsichord (Clavecin), (C minor).	1780 (?) said by B. to be his first work, with the Sonatas, No. 161.	Countess Wolf-Metternich.
177	24 Variations on Righini's air 'Vieni (*sic.* i. e. "Venni") amore,' Harpsichord (Clavecin) (D).	1790.	
178	[13] Variations on Dittersdorf's air 'Es war einmal,' PF. (A).	1792 (?).	
179	[9] Variations on Paisiello's air 'Quant' è più bello,' PF. (A).	1795.	Prince C. von Lichnowsky.
180	[6] Variations on Paisiello's duet 'Nel cor più,' PF. (G).	1795 (?) 'Perdute per la—ritrovate par L. v. B.'	
181	12 Variations on minuet [à la Viganò] from Haibel's ballet 'Le nozze disturbate,' PF. (C).	1795 (?).	
182	12 Variations on the Russian dance from Paul Wranizky's 'Waldmädchen,' for Clavecin or Pianoforte.	1796 or 1797.	Countess von Browne.
183	6 easy Variations on a Swiss air, Harpsichord or Harp (F).		
184	8 Variations on Grétry's air 'Une fièvre brûlante,' PF.		
185	10 Variations on Salieri's air 'La Stessa, la Stessissima,' Clavecin or PF.	1799.	Countess Babette de Keglevics.
186	7 Variations on Winter's quartet 'Kind willst du,' PF. (F).		
187	8 Variations on Süssmayer's trio 'Tändeln und scherzen,' PF. (F).	1799.	Countess von Browne.
188	6 very easy Variations on an original theme, PF. (G).	1800 (?).	
189	[7] Variations on 'God save the King,' PF. (C).		
190	[5] Variations on 'Rule Britannia,' PF. (D).		
191	32 Variations, PF. (C minor).	1806 (?).	
192	[8] Variations on 'Ich hab' ein kleines Hüttchen nur,' PF. (B♭).	1794 (?).	

8. WORKS FOR VOICES.

193	Bass Solo, Chorus, Orch. 'Germania!' Finale for Treitschke's Singspiel 'Gute Nachricht.'	First performance April 11, 1814.
194	Bass solo, Chorus, Orch. 'Es ist vollbracht.' Finale to Treitschke's Singspiel 'Die Ehrenpforten.'	First performance July 15, 1815.
195	'Miserere' and 'Amplius.' Dirge at B.'s funeral. Chorus of 4 eq. voices and 4 trombones. Adapted by Seyfried from two of 3 MS. Equali for trombones, written at Linz, Nov. 2, 1812.	Nov. 2, 1812.

No.	Description.	Composed.	Dedicated to
196	Cantata on the death of the Emperor Joseph II. (Feb. 20, 1790), for Solos, Chorus and Orchestra (C minor). Another Cantata (Sept. 30, 1790), 'Er schlummert,' on the accession of Leopold II.	Bonn, 1791.	
197	Song of the monks from Schiller's William Tell—'Rasch tritt der Tod.' 'In recollection of the sudden and unexpected death of our Krumpholz, May 3, 1817.' T. T. B. (C minor).	May 3, 1817.	
198	Chorus, 'O Hoffnung' (4 bars); for the Archduke Rudolph (G).	'Spring, 1818.'	
199	Cantata, S. A. B. and PF. (E♭).	'Evening of April 12, 1823,' for the birthday of Prince Lobkowitz.	
200	Cantata, 'Graf, Graf, lieber Graf.' Voices and PF. (E♭). To Count Moritz Lichnowsky.		
201	Cantata, 'Seiner kaiserlicher Hoheit' (C). To the Archduke Rudolph.	Jan. 12, 1820.	
202	Cantata (4 bars), on the arrival of Herr Schlesinger of Berlin—'Glaube und hoffe' (B♭). Comp. No. 22.	Sept. 21, 1819.	
203	Melodram for speaking voice and Harmonica, 'Du dem sie gewunden,' written for 'Duncker's Leonora Prohaska' (D).	1814.	
204	Canon a 3 to Holtzen's 'Im Arm der Liebe,' comp. Op. 52, No. 3.	1795 (?).	
205	Canon a 4, 'Ta, ta, ta, lieber Mälzel' (B♭).	Spring of 1812.	
206	Canon a 3 to Schiller's 'Kurz ist der Schmerz' (F minor), for Herr Naue.	Vienna, Nov. 23, 1813.	
207	Canon a 3 'Kurz ist der Schmerz' (F), for Spohr.	Vienna, March 3, 1815.	
208	Canon (Räthsel Canon) to Herder's 'Lerne Schweigen o Freund' (F), for Neate, Jan 16, 1816.	End of 1815 (?).	
209	Canon a 3 'Rede, rede, rede,' for Neate.	Vienna, Jan. 24, 1816.	
210	Canon a 3, Glück, Glück, zum neuen Jahr' (F), for Countess Erdödy, comp. No. 220.	Vienna, Dec. 31, 1819.	
211	Canon a 4, 'Alles Gute! Alles Schöne!' (C), for the Archduke Rudolph.	Jan. 1, 1820.	
212	Canon a 2, 'Höffmann! Höffmann! sei ja kein Höfmann' (C).	1820 (?).	
213	Canon 3 in 1, 'O Tobias!' (D minor), for Tobias Haslinger.	Baden, Sept. 10, 1821.	
214	Canon a 6, to Goethe's 'Edel sei der Mensch' (E).	1823 (?).	

No.	*Description.*	*Composed.*	*Dedicated to*
215	Canon 4 in 1, 'Schwenke dich ohne Schwänke,' for Schwenke of Hamburg.	Vienna, Nov. 17, 1824.	
216	Canon a 3, 'Kühl, nicht lau' (B♭), referring to Fr. Kuhlau.	Baden, Sept. 3, 1825.	
217	Canon a 3, 'Signor Abate!' (G minor), on Abbé Stadler.		
218	Canon a 3, 'Ewig dein' (C), perhaps for Baron Pasqualati.		
219	Canon 3 in 1, 'Ich bitt' dich,' on the scale of E♭, for Hauschka.	... ...	Dedicato al signore illustrissimo Hauschka dal suo servo L. v. B.
220	Canon (free) 4 in 1 to Goethe's Glück zum neuen Jahr,' (E♭). Comp. No. 210.		
221	Canon (Räthsel canon) 'Si non per portas' (F), to M. Schlesinger.	Vienna, Sept. 26, 1825.	
222	Canon in 8va (A), 'Souvenir pour Monsieur S. de M. Boyer, par Louis van Beethoven.	Baden, Aug. 3, 1825.	
223	25 Irish Songs, for Voices with PF. V. C.		
224	20 Irish Songs.	May (?) 1815.—*Aut.* of Nos. 6, 7, 8, 9, 11, 16, 17, 18, 20, Artaria, Vienna.	
225	12 Irish Songs.		
226	26 Welsh Songs.		
227	12 Scottish Songs.	*Aut.* No. 6, Artaria, Vienna.	
228	12 Songs of various nationality, for Voice, PF. V. C.	Nos. 2, 6, 7, 8, 11, May 1815.	
229	Song, 'Schilderung eines Mädchens.'	1781 (?).	
230	Song to Wirth's 'An einen Säugling.'		
231	Song, 'Farewell to Vienna's citizens,' to Friedelberg's words, solo.	Nov. 15, 1796.	Obristwachtmeister von Kövesdy.
232	War Song of the Austrians, to Friedelberg's words, Solo and Chorus, with PF.		
233	Song to Pfeffel's 'Der freie Mann.'	1795 (?).	
234	Opferlied, to Matthisson's 'Die Flamme lodert,' comp. op. 121 *b*.	1795 (?).	
235	Song, 'Zärtliche Liebe' to Herrosen's 'Ich liebe dich,' Voice and PF. (G). N.B. begins with second stanza.		
236	Song, 'La Partenza,' to Metastasio's 'Ecco quel fiero istante' (A).		
237	Song, 'Der Wachtelschlag' (the Quail), to Sauter's 'Horch! wie schallt's.' (F).		
238	Song, 'Als die Geliebte sich trennen wollte,' words translated by S. von Breuning from the French of G. Bernard (E♭).		
239	Arietta, to Carpani's 'In questa tomba oscura'. (A♭).	1807 (?).	

No.	Description.	Composed.	Dedicated to
240	Song, 'Andenken' to Matthisson's 'Ich denke dein' (D).		
241	Four settings of Goethe's 'Sehnsucht.' Soprano and PF. Nos. 1, 2, 4, G minor; No. 3, E♭.		
242	Song, to Reissig's 'Lied aus der Ferne'—'Als mir noch.' Voice and PF. (B♭).	1809.	
243	Song, to Reissig's 'Der Liebende'—'Welch ein wunderbares Leben.' Voice and PF. (D).		
244	Song, to Reissig's 'Der Jüngling in der Fremde'—'Der Frühling entblühet' (B♭).		
245	Song, to Reissig's 'Des Krieger's Abschied' (E♭).	1814.	
246	Song, to Reissig's 'Sehnsucht'—'Die stille Nacht.'	1815 or 1816.	
247	Song, to Stoll's 'An die Geliebte'—'O dass ich dir.' 2 versions in N.	Dec. 1811.	
248	Song (Bass), to F. R. Herrmann's 'Der Bardengeist'—'Dort auf dem hohen Felsen' (G).	Nov. 3, 1813.	
249	Song, to Treitschke's 'Ruf vom Berge'—'Wenn ich ein Vöglein wär' (A).	Dec. 3, 1816.	
250	Song, to Wessenberg's 'Das Geheimniss'—'Wo blüht das Blümchen.'	1815.	
251	Song, to Carl Lappe's 'So, oder so'—'Nord oder Sud?' (F).	1817.	
252	Song, to von Haugwitz's 'Resignation'—'Lisch aus, mein Licht!' (D).	End of 1817.	
253	Song, to Goethe's 'Abendlied unter'm gestirntem Himmel'—'Wenn die Sonne nieder sinket' (E).	March 4, 1820.	
254	Two songs to Bürger's words, 'Seufzer eines Ungeliebten,' and 'Gegenliebe.' For 'Gegenliebe,' see Op. 80.	1795 (?).	
255	Song, to Herder's 'Die laute Klage'—'Turteltaube' (C minor).	1809 (?).	
250	Song, 'Gedenke mein! ich denke dein' (E♭).		

www.ingramcontent.com/pod-product-compliance
Lightning Source LLC
Chambersburg PA
CBHW020542270326
41927CB00006B/690